PREFACE

BETTER farm methods require better buildings, not necessarily expensive ones, but buildings that are well planned and properly adapted to the work for which they are intended. A farm building should be first a property saver, second a labor saver. Farm buildings may be considered in a sense as a necesary expense, but on the other hand they should be considered in the light of an investment.

A farm barn is the farmer's factory. It is a building in which he converts raw materials into manufactured products. In a dairy stable he takes cheap feeds and manufactures them into expensive cream and butter. In feeding stables and hog pens he manufactures high priced breeding stock as well as good beef, mutton and pork out of cheap grain and cheaper roughage.

It makes a great difference in the profits whether this barn factory is so constructed that the animals may be comfortable enough to make the best possible use of the feeds given them. Profits are also seriously affected by the labor problem. Barns and stables may be so arranged as to conserve labor or to waste labor.

The object of this book is to present a great many up-to-date ideas in arranging and building in such a way as to enable farmers to take advantage of the experience of others. The author does not claim credit for the different plans and arangements offered. He has gathered them from successful barn builders and architects in many different states and in Canada.

In selecting a plan the farmer himself must be the judge of what he needs. The kind of farm building best adapted to one part of the country is not suitable for another. Two farms adjoining need different buildings, because the kind of farming differs with individuals. One farmer makes a great mistake by blindly copying what another farmer uses to advantage. Every building requires careful study to fit it carefully into the environments of the farm and the peculiarities of the man.

It is not the aim or intention of this book to induce farmers to put unnecessary money in buildings. So far as possible, utility has been combined with economy in construction. The profits in farming operations for the most part are gathered in a retail way. In this respect a farmer's business is different from commercial manufacturing concerns, because the output cannot be multiplied indefinitely. There is a limit to the production of any kind of farm product; hence, the necessity of economy in building. At the same time it pays to build well.

It will be noticed that in most cases there are plans of cheap structures, medium priced buildings and others that are thoroughly good. It does not follow that the more expensive buildings are better for the purpose than some of the cheaper ones. They are all well adapted to the uses for which they are intended. The cheaper ones will answer the purpose, but the better ones will prove more lasting and satisfactory if the farmer has the necessary means at hand to construct them. There is a great satisfaction in having good buildings, if the owner secures what he needs and gets the worth of his money.

In permanent structures, the use of concrete is recommended wherever practicable, because it is comparatively cheap, and because it is lasting. The price of lumber has almost doubled in ten years, while cement is better and cheaper than ever before. A cement floor properly laid down is there for all time, and cement walls harden with age until they become better than stone.

In building, by all means, secure the services of the best mechanics within reach. Their wages are a little higher, but they seldom spoil material, and the job is almost always more satisfactory in the end.

Judgment is necessary in buying materials; generally speaking, the best is the cheapest, but it often happens that a good second grade answers the purpose just as well, while effecting considerable saving in cash.

Farmers may save a great deal by getting ready weeks, or months, before building. Putting up even a small building runs into a great deal of work. Often the time required is more than twice as much as the estimates. By having everything on the ground confusion is avoided, as well as the unnecessary expense of getting things together in a great hurry, often at an inconvenient season.

2

A Beautiful Dairy Farm in Western New York

Department of

DAIRY
BARNS

G. C. OSBORN.

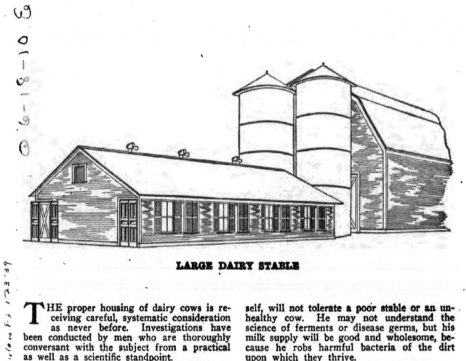

LARGE DAIRY STABLE

THE proper housing of dairy cows is receiving careful, systematic consideration as never before. Investigations have been conducted by men who are thoroughly conversant with the subject from a practical as well as a scientific standpoint.

Government milk inspectors, backed by public opinion, have established a thorough system of inspection, especially in the east. City milk supply is now traced to its source, the cows examined thoroughly for condition and health, and the stable for cleanliness. If incompetency or indifference has led the dairyman to disobey the state sanitary requirements he is not permitted to ship milk until he satisfies the inspector that he has mended his ways. This course was made necessary by the rapidly increasing volume of business which is conducted by such a cosmopolitan class of people, comprising as it does, all grades of producers, from the most progressive farmer down the line of small dairymen, to the ignorant huckster. Cleanliness is required by inspectors first, last and all the time; thus making the right start, for cleanliness leads to many virtues. A man who is particular about his utensils, his wagon, stable, cattle and himself, will not tolerate a poor stable or an unhealthy cow. He may not understand the science of ferments or disease germs, but his milk supply will be good and wholesome, because he robs harmful bacteria of the dirt upon which they thrive.

In our northern climate, warmer stables have for years occupied the attention of our best farmers and stockmen. Bank barns were the outgrowth of a desire to provide comfortable stables that were both warmer and better. The convenience of having all stock under one roof, tucked carefully away from the cold, with plenty of feed overhead at all times to find its way to mangers and food racks by gravity, proved very alluring to ambitious farmers all over the country. But animals housed in these expensive dungeons were not happy and showed their discomfiture in watery eyes, lusterless hair, hot noses and hot, feverish breath, with fretful quarelsome actions, together with their inability to grow or fatten. Too frequently, cattle thus housed, were attacked by bovine disease germs, which were materially assisted in their work of destruction by conditions so expensively, though unintentionally provided. Stockmen thought the

5

trouble was caused by too great a change in temperature by allowing the cattle to go out for an airing or for water each day; to remedy this, water buckets were added to the stable outfit and the stock confined in an abominable atmosphere for weeks at a time.

Atmospheric conditions affect animals differently. The heavy breeds of beef cattle are usually phlegmatic in disposition, paying little attention to ordinary disturbances; these suffered less in consequence, though it was noticed that they did not benefit from the quantity and quality of feed as they should. Milch cows of a highly nervous organization are more susceptible to incipient diseases caused by objectionable surroundings than any other domestic animal. Not until progressive scientific men spent much time and money in investigations and experiments was the trouble traced to its true source.

Analyzing stable atmosphere led to the detection of harmful bacteria in incredulous numbers. Scientists engaged in the work were slow to give out the result of their first investigations, thinking that the conditions under which they were working might be abnormal. Prospecting further, and while endeavoring to learn the cause, they found the conditions in these cellar stables particularly favorable to the propagation of stockmen's worst enemy. Harmful bacteria delight in a dusty atmosphere, especially when it is impregnated with moisture; when a share of the dampness comes from the moisture laden breath of animals that are obliged to breathe the same air over and over again, bacteria conditions are complete.

Bank barns are always damp and always dusty; owing to their construction, they never admit sunlight in quantities sufficient to be of use. Sunlight is destructive to all forms of harmful bacteria, therefore, a stable should admit the direct rays of the sun to every stall, if possible.

An eastern model dairy stable, combining the good qualities, while eliminating objectionable features, is shown in the acompanying plans. This stable may be built at a low cost, is warm in winter, cool in summer, and sanitary and hygienic at all times.

Location

The proper location for a dairy stable is the first consideration. Good air, good drainage, plenty of sunlight and an abundant water supply are all essential features. Fresh air and drainage may be secured by selecting an elevation; protection from cold winds by means of a tree belt or a high tight board fence. Sufficient water may be obtained in most any situation by a powerful windmill. There are other considerations, such as convenience to pasture and a short haul from the fields where forage crops are grown.

Pasture receives less consideration than it did a few years ago. North of parallel 42 there is an average of only six weeks of good pasture. Summer droughts, sandwiched in between late spring and early fall frosts, are responsible for this condition, so that a good many farmers in the east depend upon soiling crops a great deal more than they do on pasture. A runway consisting of at least a quarter of an acre for each cow is necessary for health, but the fields may be more profitably employed in raising cultivated crops.

In selecting a site the question of drainage is a very important one. If the soil is naturally dry and the slope sufficient to carry off rain water, no elaborate system of tiling will be necessary, but if there is any doubt it is better to be on the safe side.

Grading

In laying out a stable a great deal of after work may be saved by a careful survey of the grade. Manure should be removed from a dairy stable promptly every day and carted at once to the fields. By the use of a manure

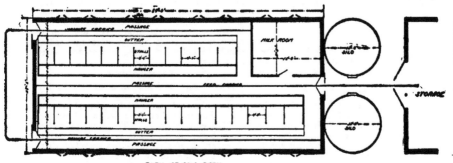

PLAN OF COW BARN.

carrier and a spreader this way of managing is cheaper, as well as better and far more profitable, than the old fashioned way of piling manure to be hauled away at some future time. In making the grade, the stable floor may be placed high enough to run the manure carrier directly out over the spreader. Calculation must also be made for carrying off the water used in flushing the gutters and in washing dairy utensils.

The intake for ventilation is another consideration before commencing work. In order to lay out the ground right, a general working drawing, showing the floor plan and another giving the profile, is necessary. Any one can work to such a plan by having a few

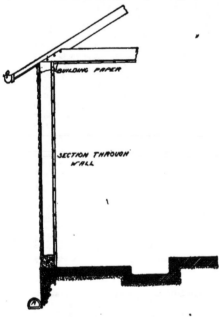

simple instruments. An A level and a few stakes of different lengths comprise about all the tools necessary besides those already in use on the farm.

Excavation

The excavation for the walls may be only deep enough to go below frost. For concrete or cement walls, make the trench just the width necessary to hold the wall material, but after the trench is dug, make a rounded recess all around the outer edge, near or on a level with the bottom, to hold a course of three inch tile. This answers the double purpose

of carrying off surplus water and preventing rats from undermining the wall. Rats will dig down at the side of the wall until they come to an obstruction; they will then follow along close to the wall, but seldom think of digging outward to get around it. The ends of the tile should terminate in the main drain above the trap.

Walls

In some parts of the country stone is plentiful and farmers prefer to lay up a stone wall, but generally speaking, a concrete wall is cheaper and better. The materials may be put together on the ground and dumped into the trenches with unskilled labor. It is only necessary to look carefully to the leveling and finishing of the job. For this purpose, a two inch plank staked carefully in position with the upper edges straight and even with the top of the wall forms a guide both for leveling and for thickness. Openings in the plank may be left for doorways and boxes built around them the right size and shape to properly hold cement sills, so that when the wall is finished the door sills will be complete and the whole thing will be in one piece.

The Floor

After the walls are finished the grading for the floor comes next in order. The profile shows the relative position of the intake for fresh air, the floor of the feeding alley, position of the cement mangers, inclines of the floor on which the cattle stand, the gutter and the walk behind the cows. Besides the cross section, the mangers and gutters incline with the length of the stable. In order to locate all these points a good many grade stakes are necessary. They are set carefully to measurement and driven down until the tops come right for the grade. It is easier to do this work before the building is erected. One point to be remembered is that the wall should not extend much above the floor for the reason that dampness will collect on the inner side or warmer side of the wall, especially in winter. Also the iron pipes designed to partition the stalls and support the ceiling should be imbedded in the cement floor when it is fresh.

Superstructure

It is cheaper to build barns and stables low because lighter material may be used in their construction. A dairy stable should have a low ceiling to facilitate ventilation. Seven feet is high enough for a ceiling, but eight feet looks better, if the stable is long, and where there are a good many cows together there is no objection to an eight foot ceiling. A good deal depends on the number of cows kept. A stable may be built on this plan to hold twenty-four cows, or it may be long enough to hold four times as many.

The principle of ventilation depends on the circulation of air. Warm air is lighter than cold air and it naturally goes up. In order to ventilate a stable, we must get animals enough in it to warm the air, which is difficult to do if there is a great deal of unnecessary head room. There is little or no circulation in a cold room. For the ventilation to work right the winter temperature in a stable should not go below 55 degrees, and you must pack the cows close together to maintain such a temperature in zero weather.

This plan takes the air in at the center in

the sill, and a two by six plate spiked on top of the studding. Building paper is nailed to the studding both inside and out. The inside is lined with matched ceiling without bead. This is to eliminate all cracks and joints as far as possible. There must be no unnecessary cracks and ledges for dust to lodge, because all stable dust is bacteria laden.

In like manner building paper is tacked to the ceiling joists and under the paper a light matched ceiling is nailed, so that the whole room is smooth all around and there are no projections or shelves of any kind to hold dust. The stall partitions are as light as possible for the same reason.

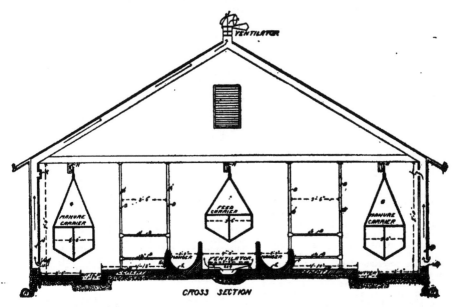

CROSS SECTION

front of the cows, where they may breathe the clean, fresh air directly from outside before it becomes contaminated. The hot breath of the cows goes to the ceiling, spreads in all directions to the sides of the room while it loads up with impurities and finally settles to the floor at the sides of the stable, where it is drawn off by the ventilators and sent out through the roof. In order for the ventilating system to work right the stable must be practically air tight around the sides and ceiling and the doors must fit well.

There is a light sill, six by six, bedded in fresh cement mortar on top of the walls, two by six studding seven feet long toe-nailed into

Door and window frames are made flush on the inside and just a light four inch casing turned to cover the joint. It is better to use a great deal of care in laying the building paper around all such places to prevent air openings. It is not intended to use the loft over this stable for storage or any purpose, but it is better to build the loft so that it may be swept occasionally to clear out the dust. A window is placed in each gable for the purpose of causing sufficient ventilation to keep the loft cool.

The outside of the stable is boarded up with patent siding and a light box cornice makes the finish at the eaves. The ventilating system is shown in the cuts. It pays to put on an eave trough whether the water is wanted for use or not, because the drip from the eaves will cause dampness, and this should be avoided. Because the building is low, a light roof is sufficient. Two by four rafters are heavy enough, if well supported by cross collar beams.

The Silo

In this plan the silos are placed at the end of the stable. If the stable is long, however, it is better to put the silos on one side near the middle, to save steps at feeding time. It is better to have two small silos than one large one. From twelve to sixteen feet in diameter is big enough for any silo. The surface may then be fed off every day and the silage kept fresh at all times.

The floor and sides of the milk room are

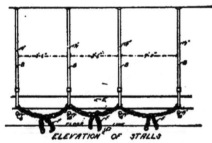

ELEVATION OF STALLS

built entirely of cement and the room has a light matched ceiling. It is provided with an open drain that connects with the main drain outside of the building, which is important, for you can see when an open drain is clean. The milk room contains a separator, scales, Babcock tester and a shelf to hold the smaller utensils, and a porcelain lined sink for washing dishes. Outside of the milk room is a rack to hold the cans, where they are turned upside down every morning in the sun. Beyond the silos and milk room is the large storage barn, where the roughage is kept and the track from the stable runs across, so the feed may be brought by an overhead track carrier. The silos are at the north end of the building and the manure is taken out through the south doors. This style of stable should be built north and south, so that the sun will shine in through all the windows.

Silo Construction

The cheapest form of a silo is the round stave construction. It is about as good as any, too, when it is well built from well seasoned lumber; in fact, it has been thoroughly demonstrated that the stave silo is a success. In New Jersey and eastern Pennsylvania, the stave silo is almost universally used. They do not last as long as some of the others. Probably the average life of a stave silo is somewhere between five and ten years. But a farmer can tear down and rebuild, because the material is comparatively cheap, and there is not much of it. In some parts of the country there is a prejudice against this form of silo. Some claim that the silage is not so good, but it would be difficult to substantiate this claim. Of course, to keep silage properly in any kind of a silo, it must be air tight. If a stave leaks at the joints, the silage will suffer, but the same may be said of any make of silo.

Some of this prejudice comes from the dairy farmers who formerly had experience with stave silos which are constructed by putting rough planks together without beveling the edges, but the way staves are made now, with bevels carefully cut to fit the circle, and provided with heavy iron hoops, and plenty of them, there is probably no better construction. Some stave silos have round tongues and grooves between the staves. This is better than a plain, straight bevel, but it is not absolutely necessary. The ends of the staves, where they butt together, are fitted with an iron tongue let into a saw cut in each end of the abutting staves.

A convenient height for a silo of this kind, is thirty-two feet made from sixteen foot stuff, but some staves must be eight feet long in order to break joints. Some builders also use twelve and four foot lengths. Most stave silos erected are bought from some manufacturer, who has a patent on some little contrivance in connection with their manufacture, but any farmer can order the material and build his own silo if he wishes to do so. The mills will cut and bevel the staves and tongue and groove them to fit any circle desired, but it is necessary to understand all the little details and see that they are properly worked out.

A good many of the patent silos have an iron framework to hold the doors. This is an advantage, inasmuch as wood gets damp and swells, but any good carpenter can bolt two timbers together in such a way as to make a good framework to hold the doors, and the saving in expense is considerable. The doors may be made loose and calked around the edges with tow, or the soft parts of corn stalks make very good calking material. In fact, there are a great many different ways to manage if a person is determined to have a silo, but it is well to remember that the doors are a particular part. The framework must be solid and there must be ample space between the doors for the hoops, and there must be plenty of good strong hoops.

Figures on all Cuts Correspond.

A—Drain tile.

B—Gas pipe 1¼ inch for stall partitions, chain ring and ceiling supports.

C—Ventilation intake.

D—Stable floor where cows stand having an incline of two inches.

E—Cement manger having an incline of ⅛ inch per ten feet.

F—Cow chains.

G—Manure carriers.

H—Car tracks, should be near the ceiling to give plenty of head room.

I—Hood ventilator, tail on opening side with counter weight to prevent friction, and allow it to turn easily. This hood does not touch the pipe but turns on a spindle which passes through the upper cross piece in the pipe and is socketed in the lower cross piece about three feet down in the pipe.

J—Ventilator shaft drawing foul air from near the floor.

K—Register for use in hot weather to draw off the hot air when stable doors are open.

L—Register that may be partially closed to regulate intake of fresh air.

M—Register to regulate the amount of draft allowed to foul air. This is one of the most important features of the system as the warmth of the stable as well as the quality of the air is controlled by it.

Q—Galv. iron gutter.

Stable for Twenty-four Cows—A101

This plan provides stabling complete for twenty-four cows with calf pen, bull pen, two box stalls, a feed room and a wash room. This plan offers the advantage of a wide driveway through the center feed alley which is a great advantage in the summer time when green feed is used for soiling purposes and hauled directly on hay racks from the fields to the cows in the stable.

There is an advantage in having a bull-pen arranged in this manner. The door at

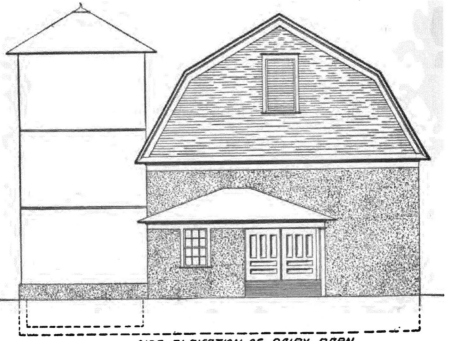

SIDE ELEVATION OF DAIRY BARN

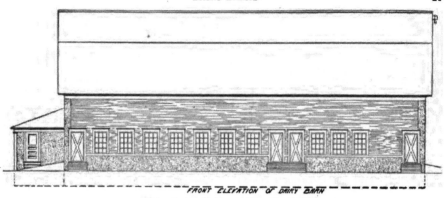

FRONT ELEVATION OF DAIRY BARN

the corner opens into the yard for exercise and the pen inside is made of one and one half inch gas pipe pickets placed five inches apart from centers. This gives about three inches in the clear between the pickets. The object in this is to let the bull see everything that is going on in the stable. It makes a bull much more contented and he is less liable to become cross. A bull needs company just as much as any other animal. A great deal of trouble has come from shutting bulls up in tight pens where

of the driveway in one end of the stable. The length of the building is eighty-four feet, but of course it could be extended if more room is desired without altering the width or the general plan.

Placing the silo near the middle of the building saves carrying the silage more

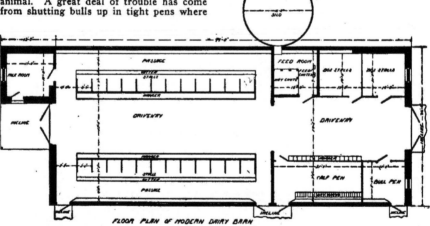

FLOOR PLAN OF MODERN DAIRY BARN

they become lonesome and morose. Box stalls are boarded to the ceiling and made as warm and as comfortable as possible.

The width of this stable is thirty-six feet, rather wider than usual, but it allows ample room for the driveway in the center and a good passageway behind the cows besides giving room enough to place the feed room, box stalls and other pens on opposite sides

than fifty feet which is a great saving of steps at feeding time. One great advantage with this stable is the number of windows. The windows extend from the ceiling to within three feet of the floor which is a great advantage in admitting sunshine. The manger in this stable is placed two inches above the floor. It is two feet wide and six inches deep and the bottom is slightly rounded. Three feet six inches are allowed for the width of the stalls with a standing floor four feet ten inches. Of course both the length and width of the stalls should be made to fit the cows. For an extra large Holstein a four feet stall with a five foot length may not be too much, but four feet ten inches by three and one half feet is big enough for most cows and it is too much for some. A perfect cow stall has never been invented. If some dairyman wishes to be honored by posterity he should get busy and invent a cow stall that will be thoroughly satisfactory under all circumstances.

The calf pen in this plan meets the views of the best dairymen who have examined it. It is twenty-one by eleven feet with a manger in front for grain feeding and a hayrack along the back wall. Individual stanchions are provided for use when feeding the calves grain or milk. It would be difficult to devise a better arrangement for calves and we all know that the calves of this year are the cows two years hence and the value of the cow depends on the quality of the calf and the feed and care given it.

A silo for twenty-eight cows should hold about one hundred and thirty tons. This amount will rather more than feed the cows during the winter, but it is a good plan to have a little silage left over to help out the green feed in the summer time. A silo sixteen feet in diameter and thirty-two feet high is very satisfactory.

The milk room is not exactly separate but it is built on the front and there are two spring doors to shut out the odors of the stable. This building provides for storage over the stable with a feed chute in one corner of the feed room. There is a large door between this feed room and the alley for the purpose of preventing dust from flying out into the stable. This feed chute is large enough so that hay, straw or any roughage may be dropped into it from above in sufficient quantity at one time. The door may then be opened and the stuff forked out. There is also a small door opening from the chute into the feed room. This is for the purpose of mixing together feed with chopped stuff in case the owner puts a cutting box overhead.

Because of the storage room above, the upper floor is made double thickness with two thicknesses of paper between. matched flooring is used and the first course nailed to the joists in the usual way, only that the dressed side is placed down. The two thicknesses of paper are then put on and the other floor laid over it and nailed over the joists, the workmen being guided by chalk lines on the paper.

Combined Barn and Covered Barnyard—A102

A great many dairymen like to have a covered barnyard for the cows to exercise in and some go so far as to keep the cows in this covered barnyard both night and day, just stabling them long enough to milk and feed grain and silage. In some parts of the country the covered barnyard is growing in favor.

The plan (A102) is designed for a bank

SIDE ELEVATION OF BARN AND YARD

sloping to the south. There is a good root cellar in the bank next to the building on the north side and the large roof surface is utilized to furnish water for the cistern. A cistern filter is placed inside the building so it won't freeze. To have nice cistern

higher than the floor in the covered barnyard. This gives an eight foot ceiling for the stable and a ten foot ceiling in the yard.

This arrangement is entirely different from the ordinary dairy barn and fits the

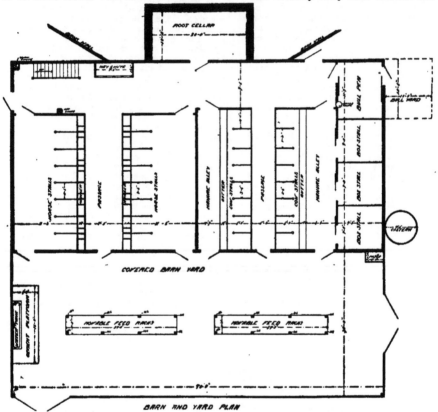

BARN AND YARD PLAN

water it is best to run it through a filter.

The feed racks in the covered barnyard are made movable to facilitate driving through at cleaning time. Mild days in winter the manure spreader is brought in at one door, loaded and taken out at the other. The racks are placed in the center under the feed shoots so the roughage from the storage above may be dropped into them with as little work as possible. With a cistern and a windmill the water tank is kept supplied all the time so the cows may run to it when they want to. The stable floor should be about two feet

class of men who do business differently. Dairymen are not alike in their methods or ideas, each one must work on his own plan. Theoretically, cows are better for having their freedom and it would be difficult to find any practical objection. Even the work is not increased if the management is what it should be. There are some splendid features about this barn. The root cellar is so situated that it may be filled from the top and the roots taken out through a door on a level with the stable floor. There are no windows in the north of the barn, the bank fills up to the top of

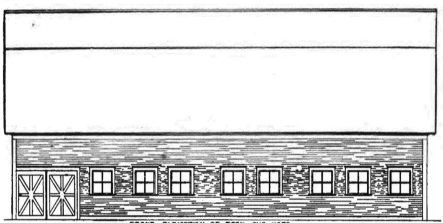

FRONT ELEVATION OF BARN AND YARD

the wall. There are double doors both for warmth and security and the yard is well arranged for exercise and there is a water bucket for the use of the bull which is supposed to be kept full from the cistern by means of a float valve.

Dairy Bank Barn—A125

An old fashioned dairy barn is shown in plan (A125). There are a good many such barns still in use in Wisconsin. Those using them say they are satisfactory under certain conditions.

One good feature about this stable is

the ventilation. To have good air in a cow stable it is absolutely necessary to have a system of ventilation. You can stable four or five cows together and depend on chance openings to provide them with oxygen, but cows in, but this is no dead open and shut reason why this stable should be built that way. One advantage of having the two manure gutters in the middle is that a cart may be driven through to remove the manure. If there is any other good reason I am not familiar with it. In these

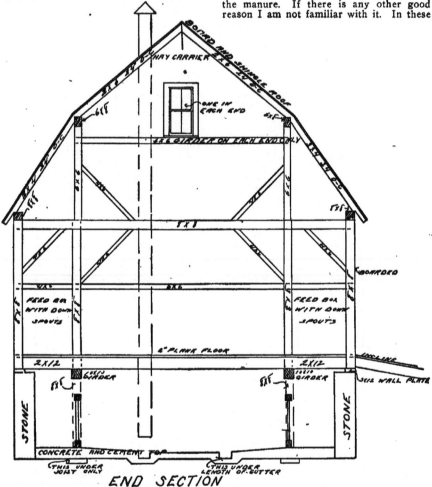

END SECTION

you cannot depend on Providence to keep your cattle alive in a large stable unless you assist a little bit.

A good many dairy men prefer to have the cows face outward. This is a matter of individual preference. Probably nine stables out of ten are made to face the Wisconsin stables the old-fashioned stanchions are used.

There is a large amount of storage over head in a barn like this, and it is a convenient barn to do the work in except in the matter of feeding the cows. It takes more steps to get around to feed the cows

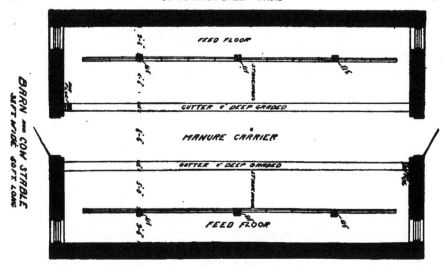

BARN and COW STABLE
24 FT. WIDE. 80 FT. LONG

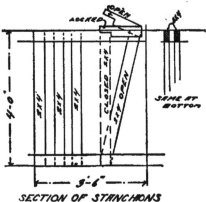

SECTION OF STANCHIONS

when they face out. This barn is backed up to a bank, preferably on the north side, where the incline may be had easily to drive in on the main floor. The horse fork is worked from the center.

One reason why stables like this are favored in the north is that they offer protection from the cold in winter and that the feed is convenient overhead so that one man can care for a lot of cows at feeding

time. Of course a silo may be used in connection with this kind of a barn just as well as with any other kind of a barn and if such barns and stables are principally constructed with a view to light and ventilation they may be made fairly sanitary and convenient.

One of the most objectionable features to this barn is the rigid stanchion. There are so many cow ties that are better that it is hard to find an excuse for building these old-fashioned clumsy affairs, but it is not necessary to condemn a stable because some of the fittings are not up-to-date. If this general plan meets with approval it is easy to supply the stalls with chain ties, swinging stanchions, or some other sanitary and humane contrivance for fastening the cows in their respective places. The profits of dairying depend so largely upon the manner in which the cows are treated that no one can overlook such matters lightly. It is to be regretted that no one has been able to invent a perfect cow stall. Some of the new stalls have many good points, but there is always some off-set. One of the best stalls made requires a certain amount of education on the part of the cow, and it is hard to teach new tricks to old cows. It requires an animal trainer to bring up a heifer in the way she should go.

DAIRY BARNS

Storage Barn with Dairy Stable Wing A136

A great many dairymen object to having feed stored over the cow stable. The mows are dusty and the dust finds its way into feet, a common size that may be found on many such farms, so that the cow stable as shown in this plan may be added to one

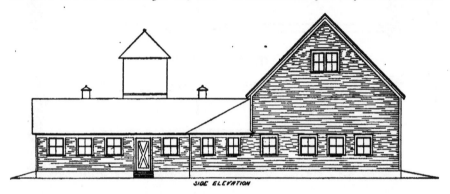

SIDE ELEVATION

the stable in spite of every precaution. On the other hand, it is absolutely necessary to have roughage within easy reach. The labor problem is a very serious one and the saving of steps at feeding time is very important. On a great many one hundred and sixty acre farms a dairy of twenty-four cows seems to fit in about right. The barn shown in this plan is forty by fifty-four of these barns without altering the original structure. Where twenty-four cows are kept about six horses will be found necessary and stabling for this many with a box stall extra is provided on the side of the barn entirely separate from the cows. There should be a good tight floor over this horse stable and it should be boarded up in front with hinged drop doors in front

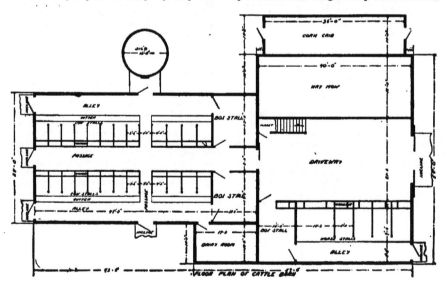

FLOOR PLAN OF CATTLE BARN

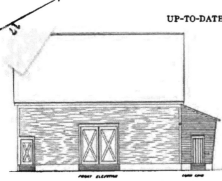

of the mangers. A hay fork may be rigged from the outside over the horse stable or an opening can be left over the driveway in the middle of the barn. The driveway would be used principally to fill the hay mow anyway because the mow starts from the ground, just the kind of a mow to hold alfalfa hay to last twenty-four cows with silage all winter. The silo in this plan is placed about half way down the side of the cow stable for convenient feeding, also to make it more accessible at feeding time. Every cow stable should have a dairy room and the dairy room should be partitioned off very carefully from the stable.

Model Cow Barn—A158

The size of this cow stable is thirty-eight feet six by one hundred and forty-two feet and it has a capacity for housing fifty-two cows. It was designed very carefully to the sewer drain so that the wash water from flooding the floors can be carried away to a safe distance.

The mangers are also connected with the

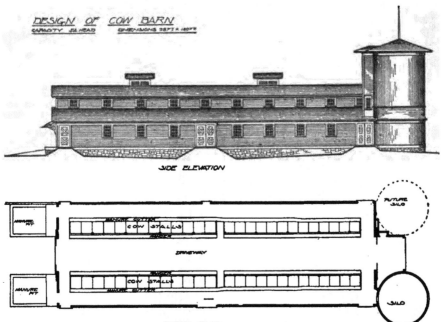

provide every comfort for a herd of thoroughbred Guernseys.

The entire floor is made of concrete, including manger and manure drains which carry the liquid manure back to the manure pits. They are also connected with the sewer so that the cows may be watered in the manger and the surplus water immediately drawn off.

A space of two feet high between the studding of the outer walls is filled in with concrete and troweled smooth with a

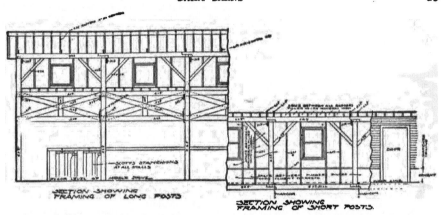

curve at the floor line to leave no chance for the collection of filth to favor the breeding of disease germs. Gas piping is used for stalls set firmly in the cement. Each stall is finished with individual wrought iron hay racks made to swing up.

There is a cement top to the concrete floors which is finished rough enough to prevent slipping and to hold the bedding. Cows in this stable face towards the center and the center aisle is wide enough to drive through with a wagon and hay-rack for hauling loose hay and fodder. The silos are located at the end, the silage be-

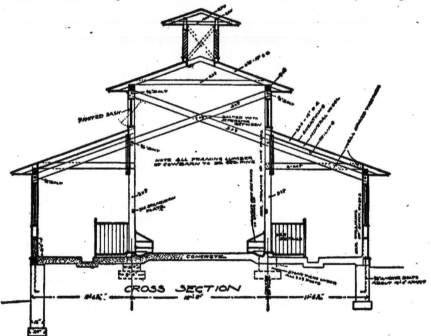

ing loaded into cars and wheeled through the feed alley to the mangers.

Light and ventilation were main features in the construction of this stable.

Careful calculations were made to secure plenty of fresh air for each animal as the sanitary conditions with such a valuable herd of animals is an important feature.

Cow Barn for Forty Cows—A159

A cow barn for the accommodation of forty cows having a feed alley of sufficient width to accommodate a wagon with a load of soiling feeds is shown in this plan. This is the cheapest and quickest way of distributing feeds to the mangers along both sides of the feed alley.

The mangers as well as the whole floor surface are built of concrete with the mangers elevated only three inches above the floor level. As cows naturally feed from the ground it is only right that the mangers should be very low down. The side of the manger nearest the cow is made almost perpendicular to prevent feed from working over amongst the bedding. But the feed alley floor is elevated and that side of the manger is rounded up to it, which makes it easy to keep the feed in the mangers and easy to kick it back when the cows shove it out, as they do while feeding.

A water faucet is placed at each end of the mangers for the purpose of watering the cows. For disposing of the water left in the manger a drain in the center with an overflow is provided. The middle posts extend from the back of the mangers and run to the roof and these are spaced to allow three stanchions between the posts.

A gutter sixteen inches wide and from five to eight inches deep is run diagonally behind the cows, starting at five feet four from the mangers at one end and finishing up at the other end five feet ten, thus making different length stalls to accommodate longer or shorter cows.

The floor of the stalls is given a slight slope from the manger back to the gutter and the surface of the floor is left rough to prevent the cows from slipping and to hold the bedding in place. There is sufficient room back of the gutter to run a truck or wheelbarrow to facilitate cleaning out the manure. The liquids of course run to the lowest point in the center of the gutters, where they are connected with a bell trap drain, whence they are carried to a catch-basin directly opposite the drain outside of the building. From this catch-basin the liquids are pumped into the distributing manure cart.

All side walls are filled in solid between the timbers with cement concrete to a height of two feet above the floor and then finished with smooth cement plaster, which makes a perfectly sanitary finish and permits the entire barn floor to be washed with a hose and flooded with water without injuring any woodwork.

Warmth and ventilation are secured by fitting the size of the stable to the number of animals and there are windows enough to admit abundant sunshine which is nature's best disinfectant. Ventilators and fresh air shafts in the walls supply a continuous stream of fresh air which can be controlled by slides. The foul air enters the shafts near the floor and rises in the walls to the triangular vent duct under the ridge of the roof and from this duct the air is exhausted through the slat ventilator towers. About 1,800 cubic feet of air space is provided for each animal

There are many good points about this stable. It is light, airy and sanitary. The different lengths of stalls give an opportunity to house large and small cattle to advantage in the same stable. Each cow knows her place and will go to it of her own accord if kindly treated. Probably the only objection is the two manure pits. In this age of hustle it does not pay to handle manure so often. The labor problem stands in the way. There are liquid absorbents to use on the stable floor to take care of the liquids and by the use of manure spreaders it is easy to haul manure directly to the field as fast as it is made. At least, this works perfectly in theory, and it works all right in practice except when snow comes too deep in winter or at certain times when the ground is too soft and muddy to drive over it. Manure is never so valuable as when drawn directly from the stable to the field. It gains nothing by being handled, run into a pit or forked over. Of course, it can be leached away from a hillside in the field, but it loses less in this way than in any other, and if a growing crop occupies the ground very little substance gets away. The plan on the opposite page shows the principal details of construction.

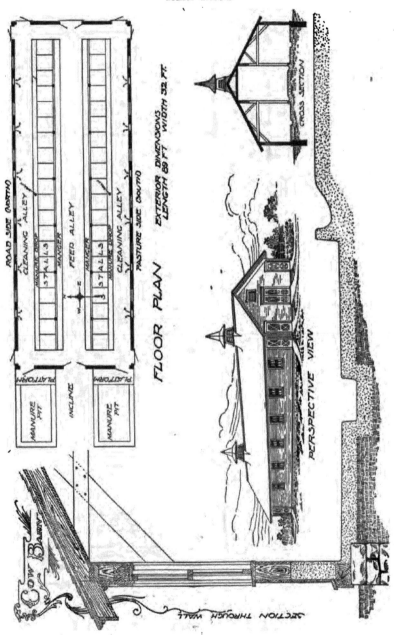

FLOOR PLAN

EXTERIOR DIMENSIONS
LENGTH 89 FT. WIDTH 32 FT.

ROAD SIDE (NORTH)
CLEANING ALLEY
MANGER
FEED ALLEY
MANGER
CLEANING ALLEY
PASTURE SIDE (SOUTH)

STALLS
STALLS

MANURE PIT
MANURE PIT
PLATFORM
PLATFORM
INCLINE

CROSS SECTION

PERSPECTIVE VIEW

SECTION THROUGH WALL

Cow Barn

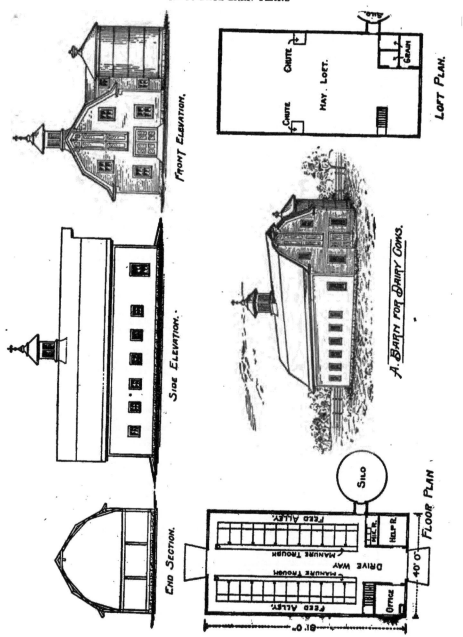

FRONT ELEVATION.

LOFT PLAN.

CHUTE

CHUTE

HAY. LOFT.

GRAIN

SILO.

SIDE ELEVATION.

A. BARN FOR DAIRY COWS.

END SECTION.

FLOOR PLAN

SILO

FEED ALLEY.

MANURE TROUGH

DRIVE WAY

MANURE TROUGH

FEED ALLEY.

HELP R.

OFFICE

40' 0"

81' 0"

Barn for Dairy Cows—A162

This cow barn is forty feet wide by eighty-one feet long and will accommodate twenty-four cows. There is a feed room, wash room for washing utensils and an office. Along one side a silo is placed near the mixing room and convenient to the feed alleys which in this stable are at the sides.

The manure gutters and floor for cleaning is in the center so that in this stable the cows face outward. This arrangement makes it easier to remove the manure and the plan is liked by some dairymen.

The balloon roof construction makes it possible to store a great deal of feed overhead. It leaves a clear space for the horse fork which works freely from one end of the building to the other. Roofs like this are comparatively new. The first ones built were not strong enough to stand heavy winds and some of them blew down, but there has been no such trouble recently. If properly braced each side forms a truss and the two trusses meet together at the peak.

There are hay chutes at the sides for putting down hay and bedding and there is a stairway at the side of the office for convenience in getting up and down.

To help out at feeding time there should be a silage carrier to run from the silo down the different alleys to distribute the feed. If a farmer wants to know the number of miles traveled about the stable it is only necessary to figure the number of trips and steps taken each feeding time, then multiply this by the number of feeds during the winter. If every dairyman would do this the location of some silos would be changed. The amount of travel will surprise those who have never thought about it. This is one reason for placing the silo at the side.

The manure alley in the center is wide enough so it is not necessary to have a pile of manure outside of the stable. Manure is worth a great deal more when it is drawn immediately from the stable to the field. This barn looks well and it is a good practical barn.

Model Dairy Building—A176.

We illustrate herewith a dairy building which is located directly west of the cow barn and so arranged that the milk can be brought from the west door of the cow barn directly to the receiving vat in the dairy building. The milk cans are unloaded from the truck onto a platform from which the milk is poured into the receiving vat from the outside of the building, thus avoiding the opening and closing of outside doors, which is very essential in order to maintain a uniform temperature in the building and to prevent the admittance of any impure air. From the receiving vat the milk

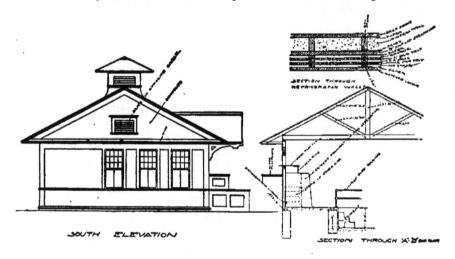

SECTION THROUGH REFRIGERATOR WALL

SOUTH ELEVATION

SECTION THROUGH A B

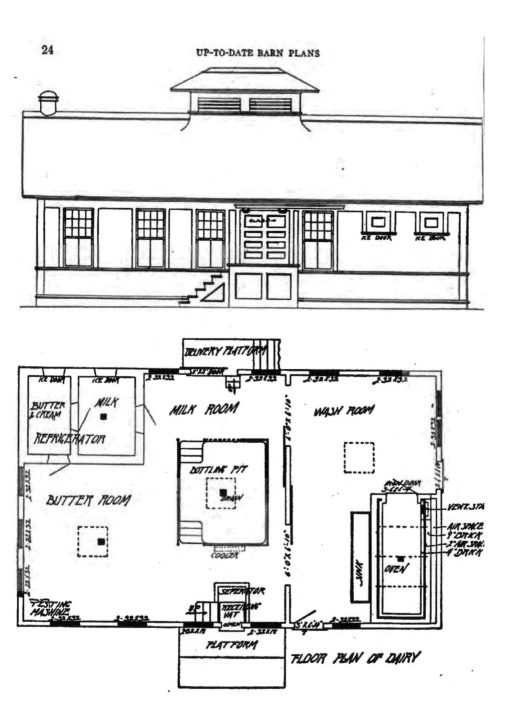

FLOOR PLAN OF DAIRY

flows by gravity through the various machines and apparatus without having to be handled by hands until it is sealed in bottles, not only for economical, but more especially for sanitary reasons.

From the receiving vat the milk flows into the separator and after the milk has been separated from the cream it is again mixed together and then flows through the cooler and into the bottling machine, which is located in a pit in the center of the milk room. The filled and sealed bottles are then placed into wooden delivery boxes for immediate delivery or else stored in the refrigerator ready for use.

In order to obtain a purely sanitary milk much depends on the cleanliness and care of the various receptacles, therefore too much emphasis cannot be placed on the washing and sterilizing. All the bottles are thoroughly washed by machines, which can do the work very thoroughly and rapidly by revolving brushes, etc., and after a thorough washing they are set into the sterilizing oven, which is equipped with steam coils and steam jets.

The butter room is located to the left of the milk room and is well equipped with the most up-to-date churns and also contains the testing machine and other apparatus. The refrigerator is divided into compartments, and is of the most approved construction.

The construction of this building is of the usual balloon type, having a stone foundation under walls of two by four-inch studding, which are sheathed and sided on the outside. Between these is placed a double thickness of heavy building paper.

Another Dairy Building—A180.

We are here illustrating a dairy building which is very complete and answers all the requirements for a country dairy. It has waterworks, power and electric light plant of sufficient capacity to supply heat, water, light and power for the various purposes required on a large dairy and stock then papered and covered with drop siding. The space between the studding of the dairy and wash rooms from the floor to the window sills are filled with concrete and then cemented on the inside, forming a cement wainscoting as well as strengthening the building. Above this cement work

ICE HOUSE   DAIRY   POWER HOUSE

farm. The building consists of three parts; the left hand wing is the ice storage house, which also contains two cold storage rooms for butter, cream, milk, etc.; the central part is the dairy containing the churn room, bottling room, washing room, etc., and the right wing is the power and pumping station.

This building is built on a concrete foundation, above which it is of the regular balloon frame construction. The walls are of two inch by six inch studding sheathed on the outside with matched sheathing, the side walls and ceiling are ceiled with beaded yellow pine ceiling. The roof is of moss green stained shingles and has large ventilators, which makes it hygienic and adds to the appearance.

The ice house is insulated with several thicknesses of hair felt, air spaces and matched sheathing and insulating, water proof paper.

The power house has a basement which contains the boilers, which are sunk below the ground level in order to admit steam pipes to run underground to the other

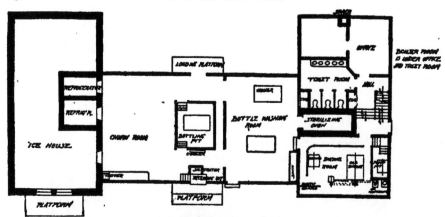

GROUND FLOOR PLAN OF DAIRY

farm buildings for heating purposes. The pumps and dynamo are run by an engine.

This dairy is large enough for one hundred cows. It is rather more expensive than most farmers would want, but the expense pays in the end because the building has every convenience to save labor. Where milk is supplied to the city trade a great deal of the profits leak away in paying for unnecessary labor. Where power can be employed to save hand labor it is the proper thing to do. The very best vats, sinks, bottle washers and sterilizers of a suitable capacity are found not only convenient but necessary. It is impossible to satisfy city customers and city inspectors, and to get a high price for milk, unless the sanitary conditions of the stables and dairy are satisfactory.

The milk put up in this dairy sells for twelve cents a quart bottle. It will readily be seen that the extra four or five cents 'on the product of a hundred cows would very soon pay for the building and all the machinery in it. A writer on agricultural questions often is criticized for recommending expense that farmers cannot afford, but the farmer himself must be the judge at such times. This is a practical dairy that is returning good profits to the owner, but there is good business management behind it, and it is managed by a graduate from an agricultural college. A dairy building, like any other factory, will not return a profit, no matter what the original cost, unless it is managed in a business way.

GENERAL

FARM BARNS

END ELEVATION OF BANK BARN

Ohio Barn, No. 146.

A STYLE of barn that is very much used in Ohio is shown in plan (A146). A peculiarity of this style of barn is what is commonly termed a double threshing floor. In some of the larger ones the threshing machine is set first on one side and then on the other for convenience in getting the grain to the machine. The bridge from the bank to the second floor must be stronger than common barn bridges because it spans the space between the barn and the bank and it leaves a runway for cattle along the bank side of the building. In this plan the cows have no stalls but are stabled in an enclosed shed with a feeding rack the whole length of the side so arranged that it may be filled from the mow above. Several removable racks for feeding grain may be placed anywhere in this shed and a water trough with an everlasting supply of good pure water will hardly freeze in here.

There are many points of convenience about a barn built after this plan, one of which is the facility for getting all around it. Gates, fences and retaining walls for the bank offer opportunities for stock pens in almost every corner without interfering with the barn proper. The entrance to the barn being overhead the whole ground space around the barn is left free to handle stock. Horses, cows, sheep and hogs may all have different quarters and be kept separate very much to the advantage of the stock and at a great saving in time. The dampness, which is a bad feature of most bank barns, is obviated in this plan because there is a circulation of air all around.

One of these barns was built on a hilly farm in southern Ohio on a site some distance from the house and about twenty feet higher, in fact the house was on one hill and the barn on another with a small ravine separating them. Two round wooden water tanks were placed near the top of the barn and these tanks were kept supplied by means of a hydraulic ram working from a running spring of pure clear water back among the hills several hundred yards from the buildings.

To facilitate cleaning the tanks one at a time they were connected at the bottom with a short pipe. In this pipe were two

The pipe that brought the supply from the spring entered the tops of both tanks in a similar way. Two valves in the cross pipe permitted the water to flow into either tank or both tanks as desired.

This arrangement of feed and outlet

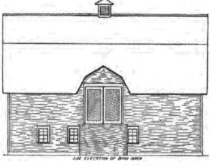

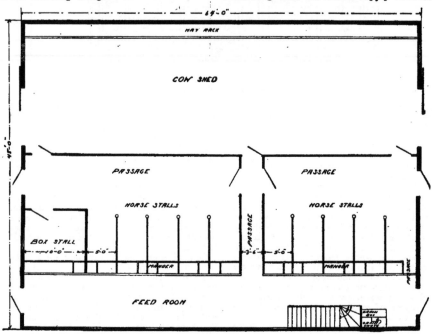

globe valves and between the valves was the outlet pipe to the house and to the stock watering trough.

pipes made provision for emptying and cleaning either tank at any time without interfering with the water supply because

FIRST FLOOR PLAN

the other tank could be continued in use. In practice it was found desirable to clean both tanks twice each year because if left longer they were inclined to become slimy.

About seventy-five head of cattle and horses were kept on the farm besides other stock and their thrift was due in great measure to the unlimited supply of good water within easy reach at all times where they could drink out of cement troughs and cast iron drinking buckets in convenient places about the stable and nearby pasture lots.

Besides supplying the stock an inch iron pipe was carried under ground to the house which was in this way supplied with hot and cold running water in the kitchen sink and in the bath room. There was also an outside hose tap for sprinkling the lawn and watering the flower beds. Another hose cock in the carriage house supplied a hose brush for washing buggies.

It might be noted that help stayed along on the farm year after year. One man grew up on the place from chore-boy and only left to get married and work a farm of his own. Farm hands are quick to appreciate modern improvements. Farmers who plan right can keep help and make money from their work.

An Octagon Barn A150

This is a cement silo with a barn built around it. The arrangement is a good one for feeding young cattle for growth rather than to fatten steers for the market. The silo is sixteen feet in diameter and thirty-two feet high with a twelve inch cement come to pitch the last silage out of the bottom.

The frame-work of the barn is very light. The silo is used to support the middle and the barn really is braced from every direction. Every side is both a brace and a tie

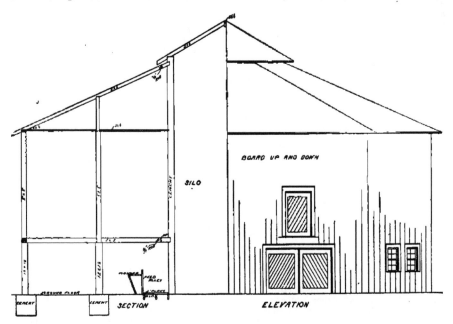

wall and a pit that reaches three feet below the surface of the ground. Three feet is deep enough to give a good solid foundation and it is deep enough when you for the next side. To prevent any possible pulling away from the silo, rods connect all the floor joists and all the rafters. This makes a circle of three quarter inch iron at the floor and again at the roof, but if the different sides of the building are well tied together there will be no getting away even if the iron rods are not used.

places next to the silo for putting both hay and straw down into the feed alley.

The mangers being next to the feed alley makes feeding as easy and convenient

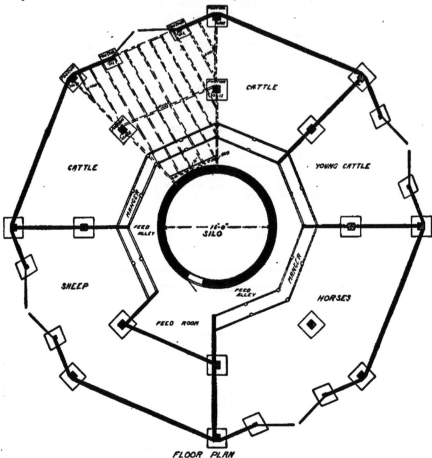

FLOOR PLAN

The octagon construction has been worked out in this plan in preference to a round barn because the construction is cheaper. The sills and other timbers are straight. The joists usually are cut square, at least there are not very many bevels and when a joist is beveled it is only on one end and the other end is cut square. It is the same with the rafters.

There is considerable room for straw and hay around the silo and it is easy to make

as it is possible to have it. Perhaps no other barn construction can offer such advantages at feeding time. The mangers hold hay, corn stalks or other roughage and the bottoms are tight for feeding corn or ensilage. The feed room in front of the silo doors is boarded to the ceiling so that ensilage enough for a full feed may be piled up out of the way of the ensilage cart. A packing box with large castors may be used for a silage cart or it may be a well built cart with heavy iron wheels and with hinged sides to drop over to the manger.

There are four entrances for convenience in getting out the manure and most of them will be used at times for letting stock in or out, especially if the barn is divided up in compartments for the different kinds of stock. Each post has a good cement footing as shown in the plan and the elevation shows the way the timbers run.

There is no floor in the bottom except the ground as it is intended to let the straw and manure accumulate, but there is a good feed room floor as this is where the work is done three or four times a day. A silo surrounded like this must be filled with a carrier. A blast stack will not work well on an incline and it is not convenient to place the cutter close to the silo, but a good carrier works all right.

The size of the silo in this plan is something to give very careful attention to. Sixteen feet is not large enough for the main dependence. Unless a person has other roughage to help out more silage capacity

will be needed where the business of stock raising is carried on for profit. Sixteen feet is given in this plan because it is a nice size to feed from. It is always better to have two small silos than one large one. The silage is fresher and the stock will eat it better. Unfortunately this style of barn does not permit of an additional silo, and the question is one that each farmer must figure out for himself. Roughly speaking, a cubic foot of silage will weigh from forty to fifty pounds and forty pounds is a maximum feed for a thousand pound cow or steer. The use of silage grows on a person and this also should be given due consideration.

Another point to consider is the increasing necessity of making the most of the corn plant. Former wasteful methods of leaving the stalks in the field to be worried into the ground later are fast becoming obsolete. Most of the value is in the stalk and leaves. When this is taken care of and fed to advantage the farmer is on the right road to securing satisfactory profits from the corn field.

Yankee Barn—A134.

A style of barn that is often seen in New England is given in plan (A134). The horses and cows occupy part of the first floor, leaving a space in one 'corner that makes a convenient storage for farm tools. There is a driveway through this part of the barn and the door is large enough to get in with a hay-rack or a grain drill.

The upper part of the barn is used almost altogether for hay storage, the hay being lifted from the driveway by a horsefork. It makes the stable much warmer to run the partitions in front of the cows and horses to the ceiling above. Unfor-

tunately, too many farmers are careless about such things and their animals often suffer in large draughty stalls.

This barn is thirty-six feet wide by sixty feet long, not very large on the ground for a farm barn, but the shape of the roof helps out very much in the storage.

It is floored over with the exception of an opening over the driveway and as this floor is only nine feet above the ground it leaves a very large loft.

There are a good many Yankee barns without so many windows, but the windows are a great advantage. It is much easier and more pleasant to do work in a light barn and the animals do better. It is difficult to account for so many dark barns, except that the fashion was established when the country was new and window lights were a great deal more expensive than they are now. Glass and sash

END ELEVATION

SIDE ELEVATION

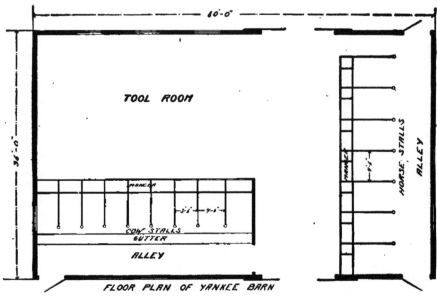

FLOOR PLAN OF YANKEE BARN

are just about as cheap as siding, there is no economy in building dark barns.

These barns are used a good deal on hay farms. Hay is more valuable in New England than it is in some other sections. They use fertilizers freely and do not keep as much stock as they should, but a good many of these farmers are making money and they, know how to enjoy life better than western men.

Horse and Cattle Barn—A115

A medium sized barn to accommodate eight cows and six horses is given in plan (A115). The size on the ground is thirty-two by forty-four, which is not very large for a farm barn, but it is not intended to be a large one. The first floor is divided into three parts; the horses occupy one, the cows another and the middle section, fifteen feet wide, is left for general purposes. It answers for a feed room, storage for a wagon or two and general barn purposes. The second floor covers the whole building with a couple of hay chutes to let down feed and straw to the horses and cattle. It hardly pays to work a horse fork in a barn of this size. The stuff may be put in by hand from the outside through doors that open down to the floor. There is no waste space in this plan, every foot is made use of to the best advantage, and the barn will be found very useful on farms where a small number of cows and about the usual number of horses are kept. The plans show the construction in detail. It may be boarded up and down or covered with siding. May be made any length.

A good feature about this barn is that it

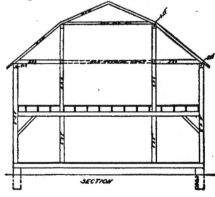

SECTION

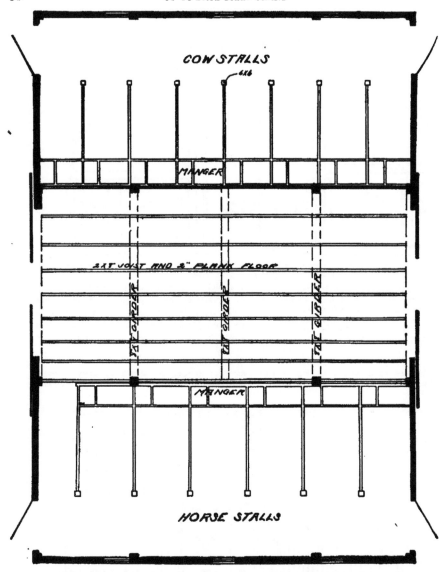

COW STALLS

4x6

MANGER

2 X 7 JOIST AND 2" PLANK FLOOR

2X7 GIRDER

2X7 GIRDER

2X7 GIRDER

MANGER

HORSE STALLS

FLOOR PLAN OF HORSE AND CATTLE BARN

can be added to without interfering with the general arrangement in any way.

It would be difficult to plan a small barn and arrange it for both horses and cows to better advantage. The plan keeps the horses and cows separate and it is easy to make con-

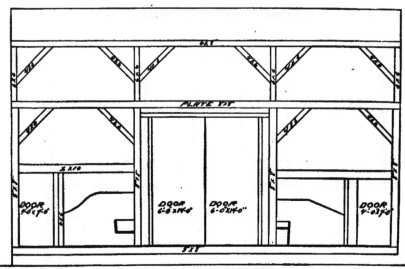

LONGITUDINAL SECTION

venient feeding arrangements for both. The large driveway in the center helps to make it a general purpose barn, which is used at threshing time, as well as a stock barn, because some of the stalls may be pressed into use for grain bins when necessary. There are many small farms where such barns come in

just right. It is necessary always in building to arrange so far as possible a building that will supply the necessary accommodation at the least possible cost. It is well also to look ahead to the time when more room will be needed.

Balloon Roofed Barn—A143

A good sized barn with a basement stable, a good threshing floor and a large storage for fodder is shown in plan (A143). The wall may be made of stone or cement

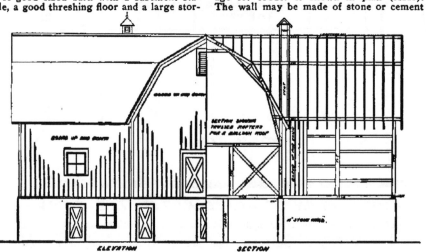

ELEVATION   *SECTION*

according to circumstances. Eight feet head room is enough for the cow stable but usually nine feet is better for a horse stable. This barn should front the south and the root house should be, if possible, in a bank on the north side and the feed alley is so arranged that a feed car may be run into the root house on a level.

It probably would be better to construct

the difficulty of lighting it properly. A good deal depends on the exposure. In this case there is a good deal of outside wall clear of the bank and the windows may be made large.

Balloon roofs are becoming quite popular in barn construction, but some of the first ones were not made strong enough and heavy winds wrecked them. This

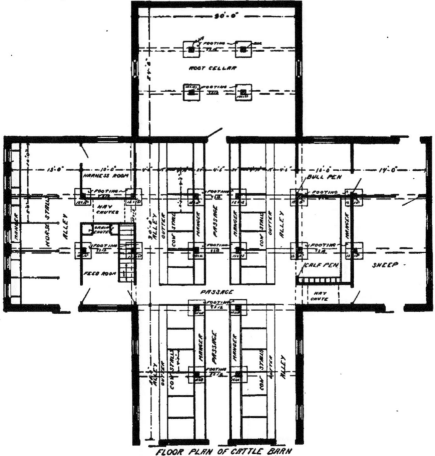

FLOOR PLAN OF CATTLE BARN

a board partition between the horse stable and the cow stable, but the calf and bull pens would be better without a partition because the air will circulate better and there will be more light in the cow stable.

One objection to a basement stable is

roof however is braced by the gables from every direction, which makes the structure a strong one.

The threshing floor is open in the center to the roof but it may be floored over at the ends if so desired. The intention is to work the horse fork from this floor; to drive in with loads from the bank at the north and back out.

It is a good plan to leave sufficient opening to run the straw carrier or stacker up to the mows above. On most farms it would be desirable to have a stack in the

to the ventilation of any stable. The air in a basement stable is seldom as good as it should be. There are two air shafts in this plan with openings near the floor.

It will be noticed that two hay chutes are provided to carry the hay down to the feed alleys. Hay chutes are a great con-

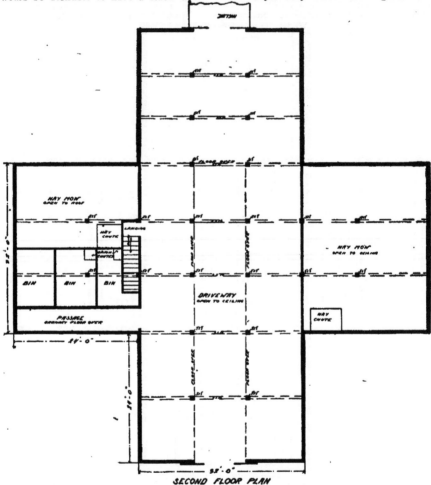

SECOND FLOOR PLAN

yard but it is just as well to put some of the straw back in the barn. A balloon roof works splendidly for this purpose. The stacker may be turned to blow the straw to the furtherest end of any gable.

It is a good plan to pay careful attention

venience but they are draughty things unless doors are provided. In putting in the upper floor timbers and joists it is a good plan to make them continuous by building them up with two inch plank so as to tie the building together in both directions.

Remember in building this barn you have no upper ties and you must support the roof from the frame below, but this is easily done because of the shape of the building.

Some farmers may need a larger granary than the one shown in the plan. In that case it may be extended to cover the whole floor in the granary wing, which would make the granary about twenty-two by thirty feet and the hay chute would pass down through it just the same.

Cyclone Barn—A126

A style of barn that has been built extensively in the west is shown in this plan. The structure is made of light timbers, but they are thoroughly braced in every direction. So solid is the frame that one half of the barn may be built and the other who farm about one hundred and sixty acres of land and keep a variety of stock. Everything necessary in a barn may be enclosed under one roof by following this plan. The cows are on one side and the horses on the other with hay storage in

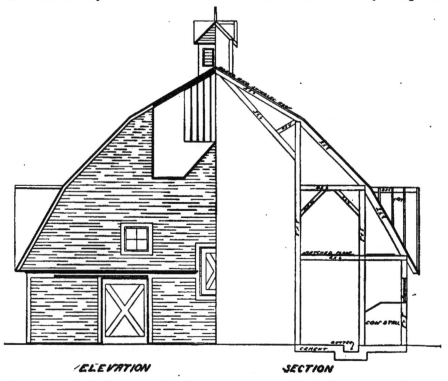

ELEVATION   *SECTION*

side added as time will permit. The frame work of each side is built on the truss plan. The roof in the center is built on the cantilever principle. Even the roof projections at the sides are built more to strengthen the structure than to add space to the mow room.

This is a kind of barn that farmers want the center and a feed room convenient to both while it is easily shut off from either.

In making the cement floors it is better to make a solid floor including the alley and reaching to the outer walls on each side. This is really necessary on the cow stable side to have it right. It is better on the horse side, then lay a plank floor

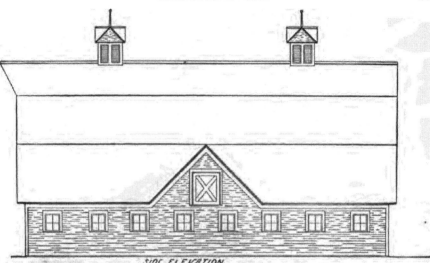

SIDE ELEVATION

over the cement in the horse stalls. This style of barn offers room for a great deal of storage and a convenient way to get rough stuff in. It is not so convenient to do threshing in a barn like this as some others but the barn is not intended

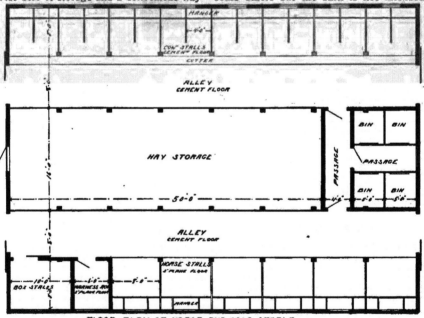

FLOOR PLAN OF HORSE AND COW STABLE

to answer every purpose. It would be difficult to make one building just exactly
right for everything. There are enough
advantages in this building to satisfy most
farmers. It is cheap considering the
amount of room enclosed, and it is especially convenient in the arrangement for the
winter.

General Purpose Barn—A190

The illustration is of a plain, neat, medium, small farm barn. The sawed oak
frame stands on brick pillars, the siding is
pine shiplap and shingles are cypress.
The barn is thirty-six by forty-eight feet
framed with five bents spaced twelve feet.

A twelve foot driveway runs through the
center with convenient stabling on both
sides. There is a corn crib in the north-

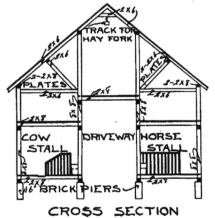

CROSS SECTION

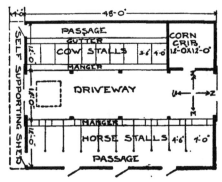

west corner but the remaining space below the mow is used for horses and cattle, giving stabling room for ten horses and six cows.

The projecting roof over the front is a great protection from storms as it covers not only the large barn doors, but both stable doors as well. There is mow room suf-ficient to hold forty tons of hay, which is put up through an opening over the driveway by means of a horse-fork. This is one of the many small general purpose barns that are found all over the middle and western part of Illinois. It is a very serviceable barn to build and one well suited to the kind of farming universally practiced through southern Illinois.

Large Bank Barn—A166

A bank barn is very desirable where a suitable location can be found but some bank barns are very inconvenient and others are damp and musty because the barn

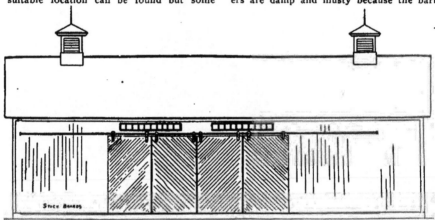

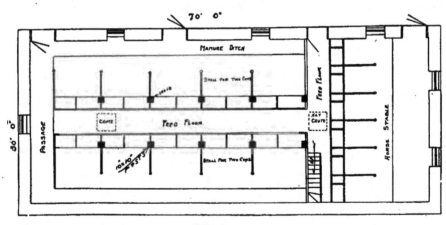

BASEMENT PLAN

is not built right. It is not absolutely necessary to build a bank barn because there is a hill on the farm. It is much better to pick out a plan which is suitable for the location than to blindly follow the lead of

enty feet long with a basement full size. The walls of the basement are of stone and the upper structure is heavy frame work braced in such a way that a horse fork could be used in the peak with a track

SIDE ELEVATION

some other farmer. A barn that is alright on one farm may be all wrong on the next farm, so much depends on the use made of it, the kind of farming and the lay of the land.

This bank barn is thirty feet wide by sev-

clear from obstruction extending from one gable to the other.

There is no objection to making this wall of cement or concrete if stone is scarce or if for any other reason a farmer prefers cement construction. This barn is placed

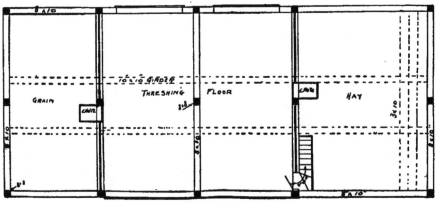

FLOOR PLAN

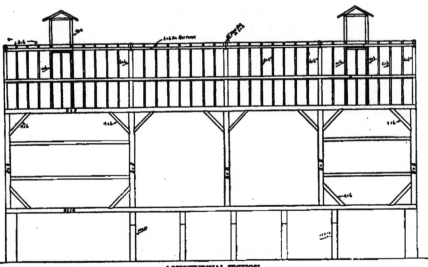

LONGITUDINAL SECTION

sideways to the bank and has two bridges leading to what is commonly called a double threshing floor on a level with the ground on the upper side. There are two doors on the opposite or south side of the barn but they are designed merely as openings for light and air as occasion requires and to run the carriers out when threshing. It is intended to build the straw stack in the yard on this lower side of the barn.

The basement is partitioned off into stables for six horses and twenty head of cattle as shown in the basement plan.

In building a barn like this it is necessary to use heavy timbers over the stable and to support them with good solid posts with good stone foundation or thoroughly well constructed cement footings solid enough to prevent settling. A good many such barns give considerable trouble in this respect but not necessarily so because it is easy to make them right in the first place.

In all stock barns, but especially where stock is kept in the basement, ventilation is of prime importance. This barn has two ventilators extending through the roof at the peak.

For convenience in feeding there are two chutes running down from the hay mow to the feed alleys on the stable floor. This double threshing floor leaves considerable room for storage of farm implements which is very important on most farms. Where the land slants like this the barn yard usually is dry but probably a little tile draining helps every yard. We seldom see a barn yard dry enough in the fall and spring. It is well to consider all these side issues when selecting the site to build in.

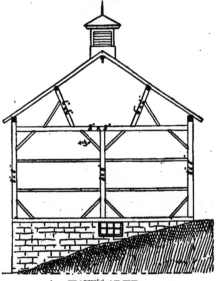

FRAMING AT END

Barn Near St. Francisville, Ill.—A188.

The accompanying is a medium large, plain and very serviceable barn on an eighty acre farm built at the very low cost of $375, the timber being furnished and most of the work done by the farmer himself who owns a small tract of timber from

of the center driveway, the horses facing the walls, and having capacity for sixteen horses.

The barn is on a foundation of natural stone pillars with earth floor, and the building is constructed to fit the hill, which

which the logs were cut, furnishing all the lumber for the frame and siding.

The barn is of red oak lumber undressed and unpainted. The frame is what is known here as the "spiked" frame, three two by eight inch plank being spiked together, making finished timber six by eight inches. The barn is sixty by forty-eight feet with twelve foot driveway lengthwise through center of main building and an inclosed twelve foot shed on the south stabling twelve dairy cows. There is a twelve foot open shed the entire width of the west end. It is twenty feet to the eaves of the main part, fourteen feet to the eaves of south cow shed and thirty-five feet to the comb. The mow above covers the entire floor, sixty by forty-eight feet, and will hold eighty tons of hay. Hay is taken into the mow from outside east end from large door just under comb, and it has modern equipment of track and hay-fork.

Horse stalls are arranged on either side

slopes to the west, east posts being shorter and west posts being longer. There is a small corn-crib in the northwest corner, and two box stalls at east end.

The cheapness of construction of this

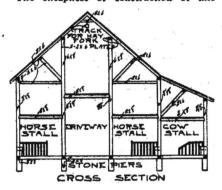

CROSS SECTION

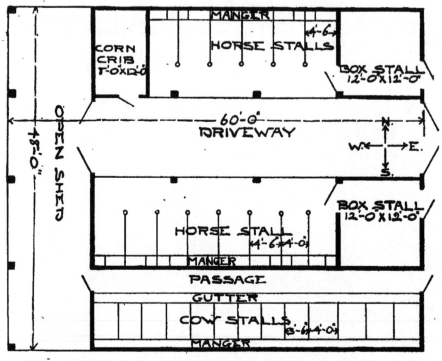

good barn exemplifies the possibilities of farm buildings construction where the farmer owns his own timber and does much of the work himself.

High Michigan Barn—A204.

This barn was built in 1903 at a cost of about $700, but the frame timbers were taken mostly from old barns and other buildings that were torn down. A good

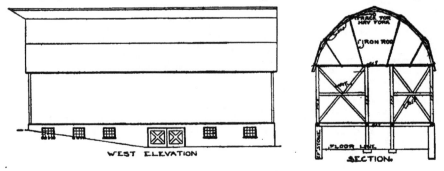

WEST ELEVATION

SECTION.

deal of the lumber also was secured in this way. The barn is eighty feet from north to south and thirty-eight feet from east to west, facing westward toward a north and south road. All the outside doors hang on hinges, all interior doors slide on rollers with tracks overhead.

The west side and north end rest on a

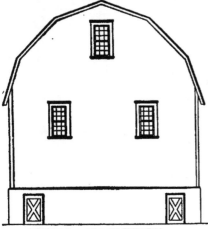

SOUTH ELEVATION

wall of faced stone two feet thick and seven feet high above ground laid in cement. The east side and south end rest on walls one foot above the surface of the ground. All the stables have cement floors. Water is furnished by a tank which is filled by an

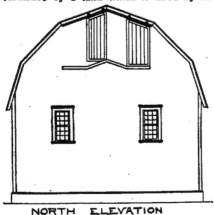

NORTH ELEVATION

underground pipe from a well and wind-mill about seventy-five feet south of the barn.

There are many features of interest about this barn. The ground floor is conveniently divided up into stables with a general shed stable in one end. This open stable has a manger the full width of the barn which may be filled from the mow above. One end of the water trough projects into this compartment, the bull and other stock drink at the other end, so the animals may be fed and watered with very little labor.

The driving floor is fourteen feet wide which is sufficient for all purposes required on this floor. It is principally used for hauling in green feeds in summer and in winter it is used mostly as a feeding alley and inside passageway. The upper floor of this barn is used for the storage of corn fodder, hay and grain. There is no thresh-ing floor so the machine is set outside, the sheaves taken from stacks and the straw blown into the barn. Large grain bins are built between mows on the second floor and the grain is hoisted through a trap door at threshing time by horse power.

A large bay at the north, forty by thirty-eight feet, extends to the roof which is filled either by horse, fork or blower, and there is a smaller bay at the south twenty-

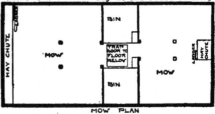

MOW PLAN

six by thirty-eight feet. The barn is equipped with a splendid fork and tackle.

An interesting feature of this barn is what is generally termed a self-supporting roof which is built in three sections, some-thing on the cantilever principle, but the trussed arches are well tied to the cross timbers below by iron rods having nuts and washers on the ends. These braces extend well out into the mows, but they are not much in the way of either filling or empty-ing the barn because of the slant of the rods and the shape of the roof.

Matched and dressed boards one and one-half inches thick are used for the floors to make them even and to make them grain proof. The roof is covered with No. 1 shingles. The barn is sided with matched

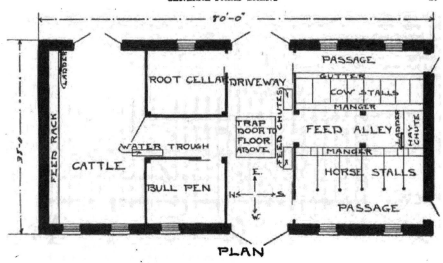

PLAN

and dressed lumber and painted two coats. The partitions also are of matched lumber.

When the first barn of this design was built in the neighborhood it was freely predicted that the first high wind would tip it over, but such a calamity has not happened.

Barn at Linn, Ill.—A194.

This is a somewhat old barn, built in 1884 at a cost of $650, the owner furnishing nearly all of the timber and lumber from his own woods. The structure is built on a hillside sloping to the west, the northwest corner showing in the photograph.

The main building is sixty feet long by

forty feet wide with a twelve foot shed on the west side and a thirty-six by thirty-six annex with mow and shed underneath on the southwest. West of the driveway running across the center of main barn over the mow floor is framed two feet above the driveway floor making a large space an advantage in building on a hillside in this way. You have warmth for the cows without being obliged to build an expensive wall around the whole barn. You don't want horses in the basement as a usual thing, and this plan has the advantage in placing them on the main floor, while annexes give accom-

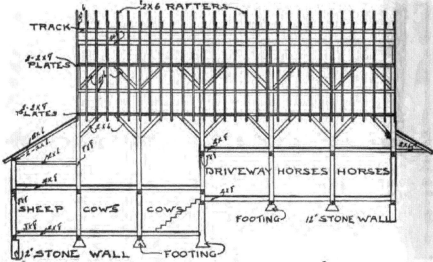

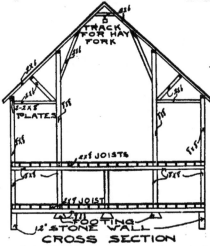

CROSS SECTION

under west shed and annex for cattle and sheep.

The east main barn is on a solid foundation of natural stone graded five feet above west shed and annex portions, making the space under the latter seven feet high. A stairway leads down from the the driveway to the sheep and cattle quarters, and feed racks and mangers extend along the sides of the same.

The lower part of east end is divided into horse stalls and corn crib, stabling regularly nine horses, with additional mangers on sides for four more in case of rush times.

Mows on either side of driveway hold fifty-five tons of hay taken up inside from driveway with fork and track. Mow space above annex is used for fodder, holding fifteen tons.

With exception of the roof the barn is built of oak timbers and lumber. The outside painted red.

This plan shows another way of utilizing a side hill to advantage in building a convenient barn. The plan is very unusual, but it is a convenient barn for all purposes. There is modation for sheep, calves or other animals. A bank barn is valuable according to the way it is built and the use made of it afterwards.

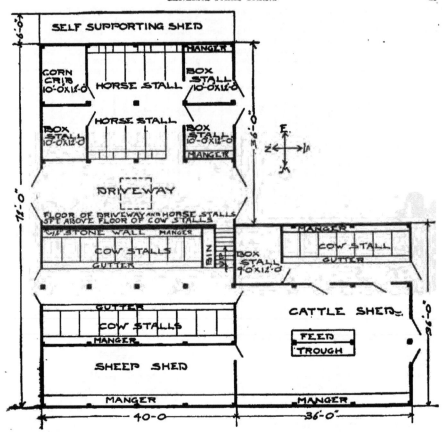

This style of building has another advantage. It is easy to drain the barn yard and to carry all drippings from the eaves and water from other sources clear of the building. It is generally understood that no barn should be placed on ground that can't be drained, but practically we are all familiar with some very disagreeable barn yards.

Barn at Mt. Carmel, Ill.—A195

The barn shown is on a one hundred and twenty acre farm near Mt. Carmel, Ill. It is simple in outline, but commodious and very serviceable.

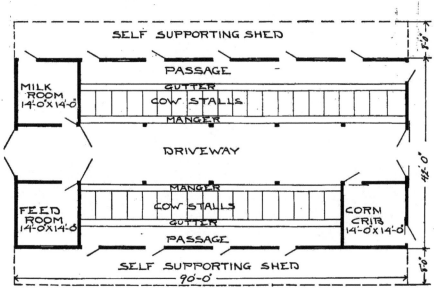

The foundation is of concrete which extends 7 ft. deep under east end of driveway forming a cellar 7x12x20 ft. in which are stored fruits, vegetables and perishable foods and feeds for both family and live stock. With rope-and-pulley device a barrel of apples or a bag of potatoes may be lowered in or drawn up from this cellar. Photograph and plan give general features of the structure, showing that the barn is intended to stable thirty-eight cows and there is provision for a small corn-crib, feed room and milk room. The idea is that later when the business grows to demand it these rooms will be removed to an outside building, or separate buildings, and the whole floor space of this barn given up to the stable proper.

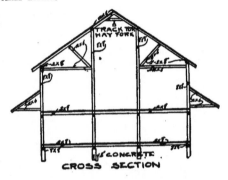

CROSS SECTION

Another Mount Carmel Barn—A186

This is a medium large, attractive and serviceable barn on the 120-acre farm of Mr. W. S. Risley, near Mt. Carmel, Ill. It stands on a solid concrete foundation wall three feet deep and eight inches wide at the top. It is eighty-four feet long, forty feet wide, twenty feet to the eaves, and thirty-eight feet to the comb. There are six bents of fourteen feet span each. The frame timbers are six by eight inches, oak stuff, and the rafters two by five inches of the same material. The siding is matched white pine painted red, and the roof is of red cedar shingles. There is a vegetable and fruit cellar under north end of driveway twelve by twenty feet by seven feet deep. The hay mow of the barn covers the entire upper floor forty by eight-four feet by twelve feet to top of side posts, and will hold about one hundred tons of hay.

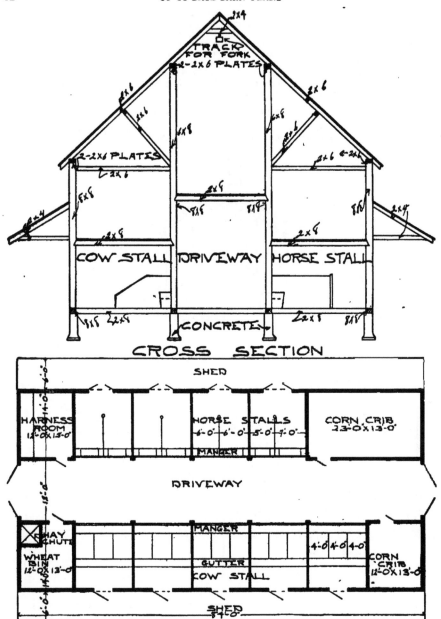

It is fitted up with modern hay fork and track, and hay is taken into the mow from either end, the openings being provided with pairs of swinging doors. Corn cribs are built in two corners as shown and they are properly ventilated.

Running full length of both sides of the barn are self-supporting six foot sheds which allows full ventilation of the stables during summer through the open. doors, but protection against both sun and rain. The barn will stable eight horses and twelve cows, the mangers all facing the long feed or driveway. The general appearance is imposing. The cost is $1,800, Mr. Risley doing his own hauling and furnishing the frame timbers from his own woods.

Large Storage Barn—A139

A barn thirty-eight by fifty feet with sta-bles underneath and a great deal of stor-age room above is shown in plan (A139). The barn should face the South with high-

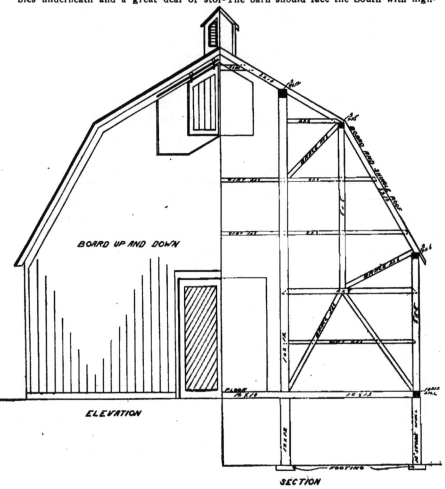

ELEVATION

SECTION

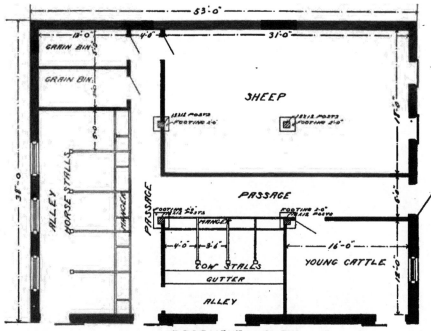

BASEMENT   PLAN

er ground at the north from which to build an incline to drive onto the first floor. From this incline hay and grain is carried to the peak with a horse fork and distributed to the different mows.

A very strong frame is shown in this plan that is well braced from the different directions. It is intended to board up and down because this is a little cheaper than siding and it is quicker to put on. When the stables are underneath and there is no necessity for a warmer construction up above the boarding up and down is about as good as anything.

The arrangement of the barn is intended for farms where not many cows are stabled. There is provision for horses, sheep and a few young cattle and there are grain bins connected with spouts from the granary on the threshing floor above. There is a good deal of storage room in this barn and it is an easy barn to do the work in. The hay from the hay chute drops on the feed room floor and the chute may be carried as high as necessary through the mow above. The size of the barn is thirty-eight feet by fifty feet on the ground, but its principal size is in its height and shape of the roof. This is a frame construction that is especially well calculated to facilitate the use of a horse fork because it leaves a

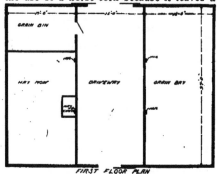

FIRST FLOOR PLAN

clear space through the center from one gable to the other. The diagonal braces tie the frame work together from every direction so each side of the roof is an independent truss so thoroughly well constructed that one half of the barn would stand alone. The manner in which the timbers are put together is a study in truss work.

This is a barn that would accommodate the stock kept on a small farm and house the crop under the same roof so conveniently that one man could do all the chores, repair farm machinery, prepare his seed for spring and have a little leisure time.

Kelser Barn—A189.

The illustration shows a very attractive and handy barn on the farm of Capt. Jas. are the cow stalls, a three foot feedway running between them.

E. Kelser, Illinois. It consists of main part twenty-eight feet wide by fifty-two feet long, eighteen feet to the eaves and thirty-five feet to the comb. On the north is a low sheep shed forty feet long by fourteen feet wide, and extending east of this is another low addition twenty-six feet long by eighteen feet wide, the north half of which is used for horse stalls, hog house and corn crib, the corn crib being built over the hog compartment. The south half of this extension is an open shed. Also an open shed extends along the east side of the main building and is equipped with mangers for six horses to be used when extra teams are at work on the farm, as at threshing time.

A driveway runs through the main building from east to west, on one side below which are horse stalls and corn crib. On either side of the driveway above are hay mows which hold about fifty tons of hay which is taken up from the center inside.

North of the middle horse stalls and crib

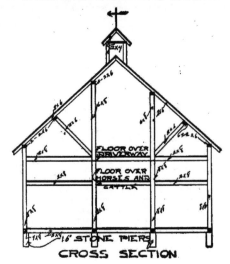

CROSS SECTION

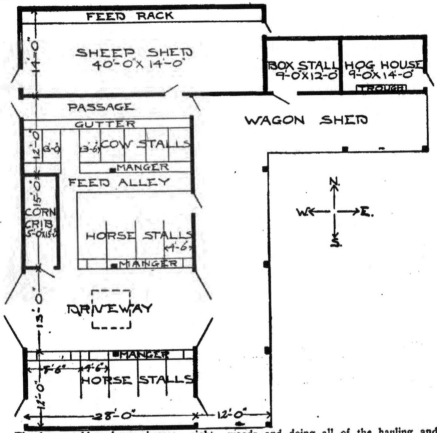

The barn stables eleven horses, eight cows, thirty sheep and ten hogs. All of the feeding can conveniently be done under one roof. It was built in 1893, the owner furnishing all the timber from his own woods and doing all of the hauling and much of the carpenter work. The barn was built at a cost of about $350 cash outlay.

Thirty-Acre Farm Barn—A169

A neat little barn that is well proportioned and suitable for a farm of twenty or thirty acres is given in these illustrations. There is a threshing floor in the middle with wide double doors in the north side as well as in the south side making a good liberal passageway through the center of the barn.

On one side of the driveway is a granary and stabling for three horses with a nine foot ceiling. A third of the barn on the other side of the driveway is made into a cow stable making seven good roomy stalls. The cow stable side has a ceiling seven feet high. Cows don't get their heads up as high as horses do and they don't need such a high ceiling. Cows keep warmer in a stable with a low ceiling and if there is plenty of chance for the air to get in and out again they have good ventilation.

It seems difficult for some livestock men

to understand this phenomenon. The reason is the air circulates more freely when it is warm. The body heat of seven cows in this stable with a low ceiling will warm the air sufficiently to keep it in circulation. If there are openings where the fresh air can get in, the foul air will find its way out and there will be a constant change.

Large stables require air shafts to carry the fowl air out, but where only a few cows are stabled it is not necessary to go to so much expense. This is a subject that will crowd itself upon the attention of farmers more every year. The increase of tuberculosis in some dairy sections is becoming alarming and it is due probably to faulty ventilation in stables. No matter what kind of a cow stable you build it is very necessary to give very careful attention to fresh air.

Both the cow stable and horse stable are boarded up in front, but barn boarding usually is not very tight. Unless matched stuff is used there is a little opening between the boards that allow for the escape of a good deal of bad air. There usually is considerable space around the doors. There are feed doors in front of the stable so the fodder may be put in from the barn floor.

It is hardly necessary to use a horse fork in a barn this size. The flooring overhead does not cover the whole of the threshing floor so that hay and grain in the sheaf is forked up by hand. It will be noticed by referring to the transverse and longitudinal sections that the timber is very carefully planned for size and length is proportion to the building. Every stick is

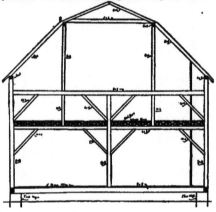

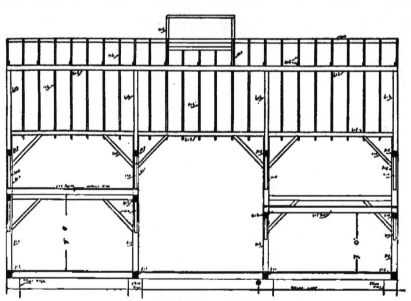

LONGITUDINAL SECTION

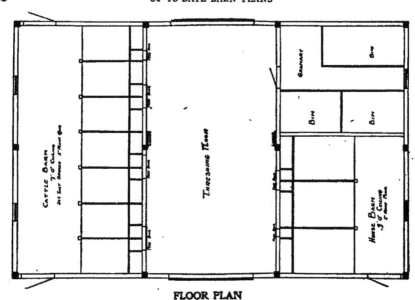

FLOOR PLAN

necessary but there is not a piece to spare. Lumber is so expensive it is necessary to economize and it pays to employ a carpenter who knows how.

Hay and Grain Barn—A167.

A long barn designed to hold a good deal of hay and grain is shown in this illustration. It is a timber frame covered with the building and projects several feet at each end. This arrangement makes it convenient to fill the barn from either end or

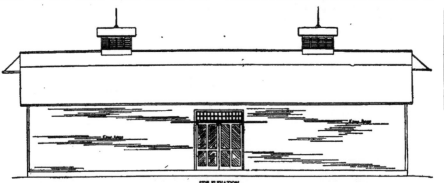

eight-inch drop siding and it is topped with a shingle roof.

The track for the hay fork is suspended from the peak by seven-eighth-inch rods and the track extends the whole length of from both ends as occasion requires. There is a driveway crosswise through the barn at the center. This driveway is floored with a two-inch plank floor, but it is not necessary to floor the other part of the building

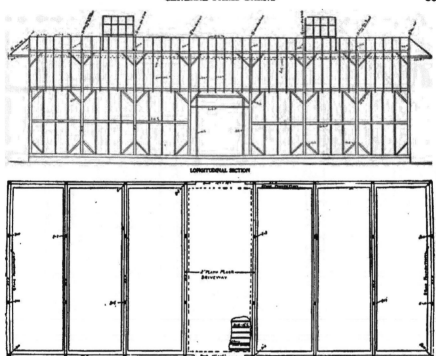

LONGITUDINAL SECTION

FLOOR PLAN

except with round poles to keep the hay and grain sheaves off the ground. Such a barn is intended more for storage on large farms where considerable grain is harvested and hay cut either to feed or for sale.

Small Practical Farm Barn—A196

This barn has been built and should be built now for $450, especially where a man is so situated that he can do most of the teaming at odd times. In size, on the ground, it is thirty-four by thirty-eight feet.

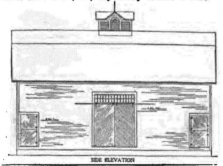

SIDE ELEVATION

SIDE ELEVATION

Open-End Barn.—A193.

A small barn for seven or eight horses and eight or nine cows is shown in plan A 193. There is also a place to tie up young cattle or calves to a feed rack. The barn is high enough to give considerable mowroom over the stable and over the open shed at the end. There are holes through the floor above to put down hay and straw in convenient places for the different feed racks.

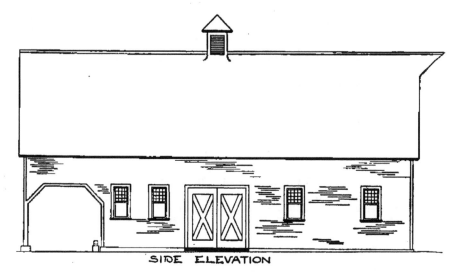

SIDE ELEVATION

END ELEVATION

The floor over the driveway is four feet higher than the floor over the stable and shed which gives room to drive in with a load of hay and pitch it off on either side. There is also provision for a horse fork to work from one end, but it hardly pays to use a horse fork in a barn as small as this when there is convenience for putting loose fodder in by hand. Where the mow room is limited it takes too long to operate a horse fork so that often a cheaper way is the old-fashioned method of handling the stuff with pitch forks.

This stable is convenient for feeding and it is convenient for handling manure. There is room in the driveway to store considerable farm machinery in the winter time and the open shed at the end will be appreciated by all the stock in stormy weather when the temperature is not too cold. A barn like this looks well and it does not cost a great deal of money, especially where the teaming may be done in the winter time and part of the material gotten at home.

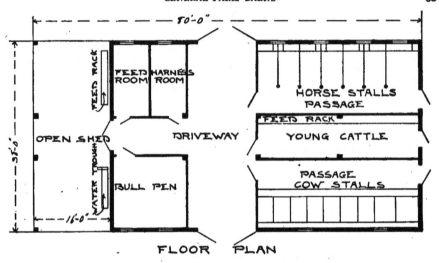

FLOOR PLAN

Barn at Naperville, Ill.—A191

The illustration is the dairy barn of an up-to-date farmer in northern Illinois. The owner stables from twenty to thirty Hol- stein dairy cows in this barn, also four to six horses in the north shed annex. The horse portion of this barn is sub-

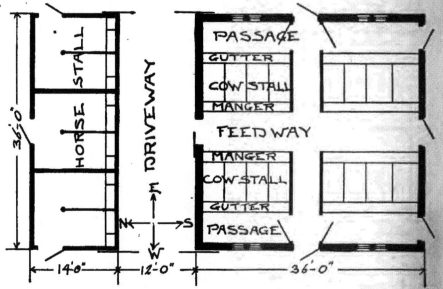

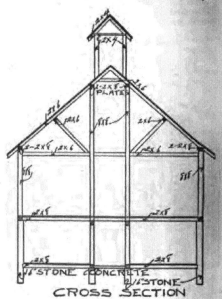

CROSS SECTION

stantially built on natural limestone foundation. Where the cows are stabled in the south thirty-six feet, the foundation runs up to the ceiling, affording greater protection for the cows.

A driveway runs across the north end of the main part, with a six by twelve foot grain and feed bin overhead at the further right hand corner of the large entrance doors. Through the center of the dairy portion running lengthwise is a feedway six foot wide, the mangers of the cows facing this. The floors of the dairy portion are concrete and wood. The framework is of heavy hemlock timber, the siding dressed battonned pine, painted red and trimmed in white. Shingles are cypress. The barn is very convenient and attractive in appearance.

In the foreground to the left is a neat tool and vehicle shed, and by the well under the windmill frame is the milk house, water from the well being used to cool the milk.

DEPARTMENT OF

HORSE BARNS

C. C. OSBORN.

Horse Barns.

FARM buildings serve their purpose best when especially adapted to the specific use required of them. Horse barns should be different from any other building on the farm. The health and comfort of horses should be the first consideration, but convenience in attending to their wants and requirements, makes a close second.

All horse stables should be well ventilated. Every farmer knows that there is a great difference in stables in this respect. Some stables are so built that you would rather keep out of them if possible because they can't be kept clean. The smell of ammonia is always present and when the doors are shut it is very disagreeable. Imagine shutting a valuable horse up in such an atmosphere at night and expect to find him in good condition in the morning. Horses are the most expensive animals on the farm and the most susceptible to disease; hence, the first consideration in a stable should be to promote the health of the horses.

A horse stable should be cool and airy in summer and it should be warm and well ventilated in winter. The floor should be made in such a manner that it will not absorb the liquids from the manure, and there should be no cracks to let these liquids down underneath to ferment and destroy the air in the building. Stable ceilings must necessarily be high enough to permit a horse to get his head up. Horses are warm animals, that is they contain body heat enough to warm a stable when conditions are as they should be.

Before starting to build put a little time on the study of ventilation. Read up on the circulation of warm air. Don't depend on others because they might not understand the particular conditions you are dealing with. It is well enough to ask advice, but get the information from different sources so that you may be able to sift the quality of your instructions sufficiently to keep the grain and discard the chaff. Don't blindly copy a stable that some one else has built without carefully considering whether it fits your requirements. A horse stable that works all right for one farmer is all wrong for another, because his horses may be larger, or has more of them, or he handles them differently. Some farmers have a lot of horses that they press into service in the summer time and turn them out in the yards and sheds to winter. Such farmers usually raise horses to sell and have more than they need at all times. Other farmers keep just what horses they need to do the work. They keep four horses or six horses the year round and they have no intention of altering their usual custom. But in either case a man can arrange a stable for a certain number of horses and build it accordingly.

In cold weather a stable big enough for six horses will not be warm enough if only two are stabled. If for any reason the stable is too large it is better to fill it up with cows in the winter for the reason that you cannot have ventilation without heat. On general principles it is more satisfactory to keep horses in a building by themselves and it is but little extra expense to do so.

When possible a horse stable should contain a carriage room that is reasonably free from dust. Every man has or should have the ambition to keep a rig for the road that is decently clean. He owes it to himself and his family to provide a respectable turnout. A farmer's family depends for change and recreation on the opportunity to get away from home by means of the horses. They are judged to a very great extent by the appearance they make. You cannot get away from the fact that a person's social standing in the community is largely arranged for them by the opinion of others. No man is independent enough to stand alone. A man's usefulness in the community depends largely upon the appearance that he and his family make on dress occasions, and the appearance in turn depends very much on the horses, harness and wagons that they use when driving on the public road.

Convenient Horse Barn—A133.

Men who keep good horses will appreciate this plan. The arrangement of the stalls is convenient and there is a good carriage room in which to keep vehicles away from the stable part and out of the dust. Every farmer who takes pride in his horses likes to have a nice rig to drive, and it is impossible to have it without conveniences for keeping it clean. With a good carriage room and a good harness room there is no excuse for dirty buggies or an unsightly harness.

A feature of this barn that should attract especial attention is the tool room. It is nine by ten feet in a front corner of the building with two good windows for light.

There is a general work bench with a vise on one end and there are boxes to hold tools and supplies on the dark side of the room. The granary will be large enough or not according to the other buildings on

it may connect with the surface drain. These depressions are sometimes made with wooden racks in the bottom and sometimes without. If intended for wooden racks the depression should have square sides just

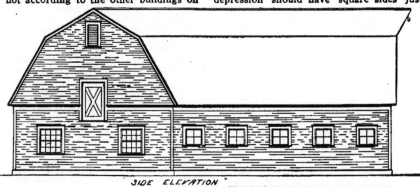

SIDE ELEVATION

the farm. Where there is a large grain barn for threshing a smaller granary in the horse barn seems to answer every purpose. The granary in this plan is placed right because it may be shut off with two doors from the stable part, still it is not so far away as to make feeding inconvenient.

There is room overhead for a good deal of hay and straw. The hay carrier will bring the stuff from the back end pretty well through to the front.

It would probably be advisable to put a cement floor in this building, the full size of the stable part and the carriage room, as well as making the carriage floor four or five inches lower in the center with a depression sloping to the outer wall where

FRONT ELEVATION

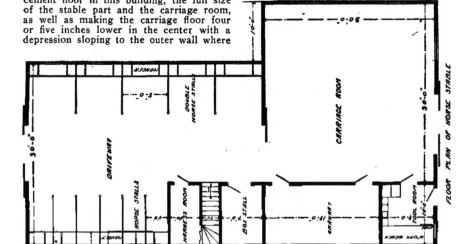

deep enough to bring the rack level with the top of the main floor.

The advantage of a rack is that buggies may be washed and the water left to drain away, whereas if you simply have a rounded depression you are standing in water from a quarter of an inch to an inch deep while washing the rigs. If you want to wear rubber boots this would not be an objection and an open depression is easier to clean, in fact it is but a few minutes' work to brush the water out with a stable sweep. After the work is done a rack would probably remain in place for some time waiting for an opportunity to lift it out and clean the pit. Cement floors in stables are worth a great deal just to prevent rats from working mischief.

Plain Horse Barn—A161.

A plain straight-away horse barn with ten single stalls, five box stalls, feed room, harness room and vehicle room with a wash platform in the center is given in this

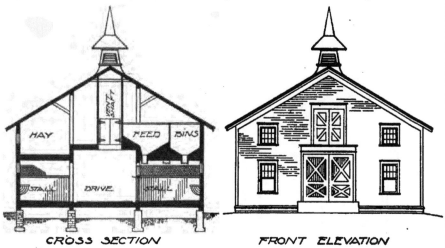

CROSS SECTION   FRONT ELEVATION

PERSPECTIVE VIEW

H. H. NIEMANN, DEL.

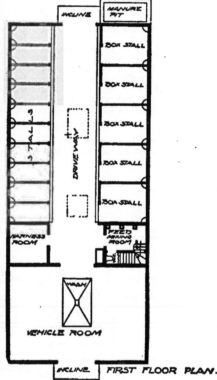

FIRST FLOOR PLAN.

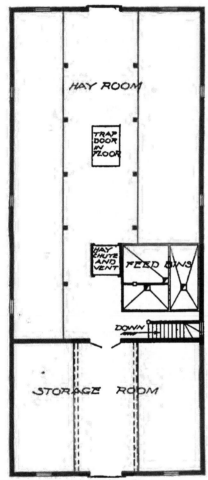

SECOND FLOOR PLAN

plan. There is a driveway through the center wide enough to admit a load of hay or a load of straw, if so desired, but there are doors opening outside in the gable to pitch in hay and straw, either by hand or horse fork, so it would not be necessary ordinarily to drive inside with a bulky load, but a good passageway between horse stalls is a great convenience anyway.

This barn will easily accommodate fifteen horses and it will hold feed enough to supply them for a long time. The building is thirty-seven feet wide by sixty-eight feet long. It is set on a stone foundation with two rows of stone piers supporting the floor joists and posts which run to purlin plates.

There is a large vent shaft running from the stable ceiling to and through the hay mow with doors for throwing down hay or fodder as well as for ventilation. Grain in sacks can be hoisted up this ventilator shaft and conveniently dumped into feed bins which have hopper bottoms and spouts leading to the mixing room below.

In the driveway at one side of the mixing room door is a water supply pipe and watering trough with a hose connection to supply water to the wash room on the floor of the vehicle room.

The stalls are floored with a double thickness of oak flooring one and three-quarter inches thick slightly sloping to cast iron gutters, which run the entire length of the stall room on each side of the driveway. The first thickness of these stall floors is laid in hot tar, then two thicknesses of tar roofing felt is put on being well mopped over with tar, and this covered with the upper thickness of oak one and three-quarter inch flooring.

Where a great many horses are to be fed overhead feed bins are a great convenience. The bottoms may be made hopper shape as shown in the plan, or they may be level. A hopper, of course, is best, but with a flat bottom a little accumulation of grain around the edges at the bottom is all that remains when the grain stops running down the spout, and flat bottom bins are cheaper.

The main entrance doors are both wide and high. Unless the door is large enough it is sometimes difficult to get out. The door must have a good height because you want room for a carriage or a top-buggy. We all have had experience in catching a buggy top on the lintel of a low door way. It seems to be the proper occasion for saying things. No builder likes to have such remarks made about him.

There is a good row of box stalls It is difficult to plan a decent sized box stall in a small stable. They run into room too fast. Nothing looks so comfortable for a good horse as a roomy box stall. If the horses had their way about it there would be more box stalls, but it really requires about three times as much room to stable horse in this way. No man begrudges the room, but most men don't like to put up money enough to enclose it properly.

The ideal arrangement for stabling a horse is a big box stall with a good sized window for light and a door cut in half so that the upper part may be left open during the daytime to let the horse look out. A box stall shut up tight is a prison for a horse, they like to see things as well as other folks.

Some box stalls are fitted with rubbing boards. These consist of planks about two inches thick turned edgewise to the horse and fastened to the sides of the stall just low enough down so the horse can't rub his tail. A box stall needs no floor and there should be no feed rack or manger. A box on the ground to feed oats in is all the manger necessary. The hay should be put in at frequent intervals in small quantities placed lightly on the floor or bedding against the side of the stall. This way of feeding has often cured horses of chronic indigestion.

In building a stable it is a great deal better to find out all these little details and build accordingly. There are several reasons why box stalls are better than standing stalls with mangers. A horse loves his freedom. To understand this it is only necessary to watch a horse when you take the bridle or halter off.

One great defect in horse stalls as you ordinarily see them is lack of ventilation. It is quite common to see the inner walls of a stable in winter white with frost. The frost wouldn't be there if the stable was dry as it should be. It is not necessary to put in an elaborate system of ventilating pipes in a small stable. The windows and doors are sufficient if they are managed right. The breath of one or two horses is easily taken care of, but even in small stables such things often are neglected.

In this barn the carriage room is closed off from the stable which is right. The odor from the stable is a damage to the carriages and to the rugs. The stable should be warmer than the carriage room so the door works right from both sides.

Storage for Grain.—A130.

A cheap little stable and granary with considerable loft room may be built after plan A 130. It is twenty-one by thirty-four feet including the implement shed at the end. This little barn is intended for a

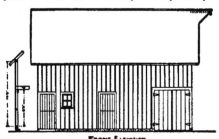

FRONT ELEVATION

FLOOR PLAN

small farm where a little grain is grown and fed to horses that are used partly for farm work and partly perhaps for teaming for hire.

There is an eight-foot ceiling over the stable and over the grain bins and a ten-foot ceiling over the machinery room, because a stable is warmer with a low ceiling and eight feet is not high enough to accommodate all kinds of farm machinery.

On some small farms this shed room would not be necessary for storage purposes, but it would be very handy to drive loads in at night for safe keeping. The opposite doors make it very handy to drive

through which is much better than being obliged to back out with a heavy load. The grain bins also are filled from this shed by drawing the sacks directly from the thrashing machine and dumping through the openings shown in the plan. Each opening is three feet square and is closed with a swinging sash fitted with four lights of glass.

This little barn is quite different from the ordinary, but it is not necessary to build a barn just exactly like some other barn. A barn like other farm implements should be built for a purpose and carefully arranged to fit the case in order the greatest value for the money paid out.

Eight Horse Stable—A124.

A small cheap horse stable is shown in plan (A124). It sometimes happens that a separate stable for horses is necessary because of the manner in which the other buildings are constructed and occupied. This little stable will accommodate eight horses and there is room enough overhead to hold the straw for bedding, but it would be necessary to provide the feed from some

SIDE ELEVATION

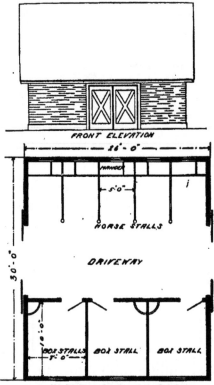

FRONT ELEVATION

HORSE STALLS

DRIVEWAY

BOX STALLS   BOX STALL   BOX STALL

FLOOR PLAN OF BARN

near-by storage. It is not necessary to put a floor in this stable unless it be on the side where the open stalls are built. But a good many horse stalls have stiff clay pounded in and there are plenty of horse men who prefer such stable bottoms. They are all right if kept in good condition. As the material costs little or nothing a man can afford to put a little work on repairs occasionally.

In making a clay floor the clay should be selected with a great deal of care. Some clays will pack so hard that they are almost equal to cement, while others soften easily or pound into dust. Generally speaking, a very stiff clay makes the best bottom. Sometimes an addition of wood ashes will help and sometimes a little lime will mix with the clay to advantage. By trying different compositions in a small way before the floor is wanted the

proper mixture may be arrived at. No definite instructions can be given, because materials differ in composition. Stones are not to be recommended, but sometimes sifted gravel in sizes not larger than a grain of corn will work in to advantage.

Village Stable With Cellar—A116.

A very neat attractive stable for a city or village is here given. A good stone wall is laid down below frost, or it may be carried a little deeper and the part under the carriage room excavated for a cellar, but in this case a retaining wall would be necessary on the stable side because the box stalls are supposed to have an earth floor, but no matter how you floor the stalls you want the retaining wall just the same, because you don't want horses over a cellar.

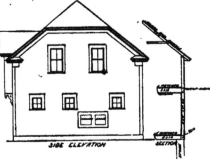

FRONT ELEVATION

Cellars under stables are not as common as they should be. With a good cellar you can store carrots and turnips in the fall for winter feeding, and they are very valuable for horses. Some horse men consider

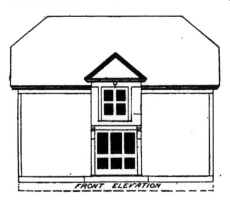

FIRST FLOOR PLAN

a bushel of carrots as valuable as a bushel of oats to feed to a horse in the winter time, not that the carrots supply as much nutriment as the oats, but because their feed value is considerable and because of

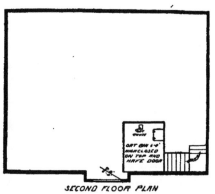

SIDE ELEVATION

their laxative principles and their health giving qualities. If a stable is supplied with a good cellar it is an inducement to better feeding. The cellar may be filled

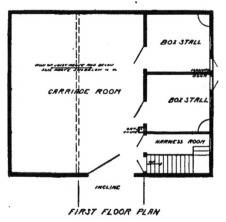

SECOND FLOOR PLAN

through a trap door in the carriage room floor and a stairway made to it under the stair that goes up to the overhead mow.

The elevation of this barn is pleasing because it is not exactly plain. Still there is not much additional expense in building a roof like this or in the little projection from the upper door in front. This style of roof and finish helps to give the barn a rather solid appearance. Of course, all village stables should correspond in general architectural effect to the house, because usually there are only two buildings on the lot and it is fit that they should appear architecturally alike.

Another Cheap Stable—A132.

Plan (A132) is a small carriage house which may be built at very little expense. It often happens that a man wants to keep a horse for his own driving when he don't care to put a great deal of expense on the stable. It is a mistake in such cases to build a cheap looking affair, because a man is never satisfied with it and it injures a person's property. It is just as easy to build an attractive stable, one that is well

er's ambition.

Here is a stable that costs very little to build, but you never would know it, especially if it is neatly painted and nicely kept both inside and outside, as it should be. There is sometimes more genuine satis-

FRONT ELEVATION.

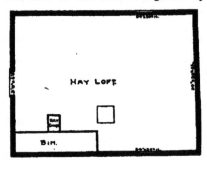

SIDE ELEVATION.

faction in a cheap building well cared for than in an expensive structure that is permitted to go to seed.

The size of this barn is eighteen by

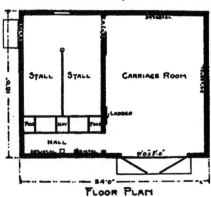

FLOOR PLAN

SECOND FLOOR.

proportioned and well designed, because if rightly laid out it costs but little more than a poor looking affair that has a cheap appearance. It is alright to build cheap if nobody finds it out, but we often see miserable structures that give away the own-

twenty-four feet. Its attractive appearance is due more to the shape of the roof than to the general design or to any other one feature. All village barns should be placed carefully on the lot to look well and so they will not annoy the neighbors.

Gothic Barn—A181.

If the horse barn is near the house and if the house has a steep roof the barn should have a similar roof to be in keeping. We often see a house of one style and the other buildings nearby built on entirely different lines. If the house is new and the other buildings old there is some excuse for such incongruity, but in most cases the house is built first and the barn is added to the lot some years afterwards. In the meantime some architectural fad has taken possession of the neighborhood and every building erected must bear the marks of the new fashion.

There is too little originality in building. It is much easier to follow the local trend than it is to think out a plan that is suitable for individual needs. In offering this barn plan it is with the idea that there are many locations where the style of building and the shape of the roof will match the house and other surroundings better than any other plan.

A roof like this is not economical to build if the owner is influenced, especially by dollars and cents, but there is a style about it that shows up well for the amount of money it costs. There is a great deal in appearance. When we have things right we have something to appreciate for a long time to come. If the house has a steep roof we cannot tolerate a barn with a main roof that is, say one-third pitch and a lean-to that is even less.

If the mischief has been done conditions may be somewhat improved by moving the barn well back out of the way and having it covered with vines or screened in some way so it is not obtrusive. But there is something wrong with a man who will build a gothic house and a barn with a flat roof on the same lot. His ideas have been dwarfed in some direction. His property shows it because it does not balance up right.

A lot with its buildings must be one homogeneous whole or it shows at once that it has not been arranged rightly. A village stable may be made an ornament to the property or a damage to the owner and an eyesore in the neighborhood. Neighbors often say unkind things about the owner of the barn on the next lot. Not always on account of the looks of the thing, they may be aggravated by the perfume or noise of the chickens when they want to sleep in the morning.

A good many folks don't like neighbors,

FRONT ELEVATION   SIDE ELEVATION.

DESIGN FOR A SMALL BARN   WITH FOUR STALLS

and it is generally for some such reason, but neighbors are necessary and the neighbors sometimes build barns and they don't always keep them nicely. It requires a level-headed man to lay out a lot to the best advantage and to put up buildings in such a way that no one can find fault with them.

may be easily locked shut. It is a good plan to have some little cupboard like this that may be locked when occasion requires it. In almost every stable medicines are kept, and they should be out of the way of children. It is a splendid precaution to keep medicine bottles locked up. A great many accidents have come just from carelessness in this respect.

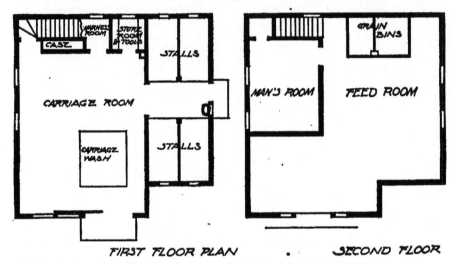

FIRST FLOOR PLAN   SECOND FLOOR

There is something about the arrangement of this barn inside that will appeal to every orderly person. The stalls are right for convenience, both in handling the horses and for cleaning the stable. The carriage room is quite large and convenient with two store rooms, one for general garden tools with a place for a small workbench on one side, a necessity in almost any village lot where a man is kept to do the chores. The other store-room is intended for harness. There is also a case which comes in very handy to keep the smaller things and those that are valuable. The glass doors slide past each other and

Every village stable that is large enough should have a room for the man, it may not be necessary at all times, but the time probably will come when this room will be found very useful. In this case it is built in one of the large gables where the roof is steep enough to lath and plaster right on the rafters. It is a case of building a roof and a side at the same time and it makes a saving in expense in one way or the other. You either don't pay for the roof or you don't pay for the side of the room.

English Carriage House—A99.

Small artistic stables are more common in England than they are in the United States, possibly because the country is older and the people have had more time to develop an artistic taste in such matters. An English gentleman likes to keep his cob and cart. He wants a good smart turn-out that presents a respectable if not a dashing

appearance; then he likes to have things in keeping at home, so he maintains a very neat carriage house and stable.

Some of these carriage houses are older than the proprietor but you would never know it to look at them. They are kept in such repair and they nestle amongst the hedges and trees in such a pretty homelike way that you never think about their age or intrinsic value. You get the impression at once that they are proper and proper goes a long way in England. You don't

father or their double great uncle did the same thing long before they were born, so all they have to do is to follow precedent.

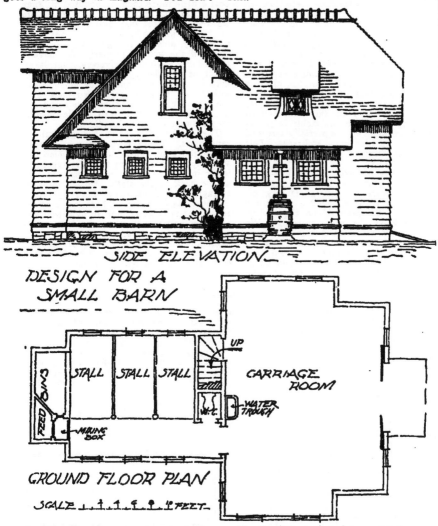

SIDE ELEVATION

DESIGN FOR A SMALL BARN

GROUND FLOOR PLAN

SCALE ⊥ ⊥ ⊥ ⊥ ⊥ ⊥ FEET

wonder that they have very neat stables just the right size and that they appear modestly retiring away to the back end of the pretty garden. It just seems to come natural. Their great, great grand-

The English carriage house of today was built after hundreds of years of experimenting until the location of every plank, the size and direction of every door and window was determined without any further question in regard to the possibility of the slightest improvement. It is put back on the lot in the furtherest corner from the house. The approach to it is through an arched or pillored opening in a beautifully well-kept hedge. The driveway is not straight. English gardeners keep just as far away from straight lines as they possibly can. Somebody discovered in the time of King Alfred that curved paths and roadways in gardens were proper. Some old enthusiast went a step too far and got them crooked. This was frowned upon for a century or two until succeeding generations pulled some of the kinks out by injecting a few liberal doses of English conservatism so that now after a good many generations the driveway from the lane through the back of the lot to the stable is gently curved. The stable also is partially screened from view by hedges, vines and trees: This is proper in England, it is good sense in any other country.

The difficulty of doing things just right in the United States is that we are in too much of a hurry to get satisfactory results. We get ready to build a stable one day and have the material on the ground before breakfast the next morning. We haven't decided where to put the thing so we go out with the carpenter harboring the idea that his time is going on and that while we detain him he is not engaged in sawing or hammering. For economy sake we must decide instantly. The street line is guessed at and the barn placed just a little inside. After it is up and the workmen have gone there is plenty of time to think it over and regret not having done some things differently, but the bar is up now, it has cost a little more than we counted on, they always do cost more than we expect, and we always expect they will when we start in, but at any rate, we haven't any time or money now to change things or even level off the ground properly. We haven't figured on a curved driveway, that is all nonsense, but we lay down some planks to keep us out of the mud. The finish is not satisfactory to ourselves or anybody else, but we have a barn and we have secured it in characteristic American hustle fashion so we ought to be satisfied.

The plan (A99) shows the general arrangement. There is a room partitioned off in the gable upstairs for the man. A stairway going up from the carriage room lands in this upper room. The feed bins at the back of the stalls connect with the storage bin on the upper floor by means of spouts as indicated. There is a carriage room that is large enough to look well and to accommodate a number of vehicles. Instead of having a harness room there are pegs for harness in a corner of the carriage room and the harness is covered with curtains hung to a wire overhead.

Horse Shed—A121.

On farms where a number of brood mares are kept and colts of all ages are coming along, it is much better to have a separate shed for winter feeding for the colts than to let them run at large among the cattle. One colt might not do much damage in the general barnyard, but colts are mischievous and one teaches another.

A light shed may be built on this plan, which is fifteen by thirty-four feet, at very little expense. It should front on the stack yard and face the south if possible. For economy it is placed on cedar posts let in the ground below frost, but it should be thoroughly banked around the back and

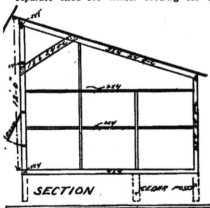

SECTION   CEDAR POST

HORSE SHED

ends in the fall to keep out the cold winds. In banking up a shed like this set a board all around the outside to keep the earth away from the building proper. Fit the board nicely so there are no chinks to let in cold drafts.

Three Story Horse Barn—A117.

A bank barn for horses, thirty-two by thirty-six feet, is shown in this plan. The stable is in the basement and on the main floor there is a driveway with a corn crib on one side and bins for grain on the other. Above this main floor is mow room bins above and the corn crib as well as hay mow by means of chutes. The hay and oat

SIDE ELEVATION

FRONT ELEVATION

chutes are perpendicular and pass straight down from the loft and from the grain bin to the feed room below. But the corn chute is built diagonally across under the main driveway floor to carry it over to the

other. Above this main floor is mow room for hay and straw.

This barn will furnish stabling for eleven horses in the basement, besides a feed room which is connected with the grain

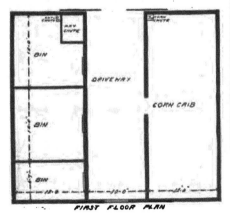

FIRST FLOOR PLAN

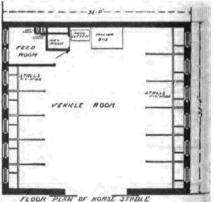

FLOOR PLAN OF HORSE STABLE

feed room. The reason for this is that all feed rooms should be shut off from the stable with a good door. Most of us have had experience with horses getting loose at night and eating more grain than was good for them. This corn chute is twelve by fourteen inches, which is small enough, considering that it is a slanting chute. All grain chutes when built in this way require to be larger than when placed vertical, because there is more friction in the passage of the grain in coming down.

The corn crib is ventilated on three sides by using narrow strips nailed to cleats slanting outward. This will answer for corn that is reasonably dry, but unless the weather is favorable it is not a good plan to fill a bin like this full of corn without some kind of a ventilator in the middle.

Small Barn With Cement Floor—A112.

This barn is twenty-two feet wide by thirty-four feet long and has a cement floor a plank floor running lengthwise of the stall over the cement. These planks are not

cushioned with cinders the whole size of the building, but the standing stalls have fastened except to two cross pieces—the one under the manger is a two by four laid

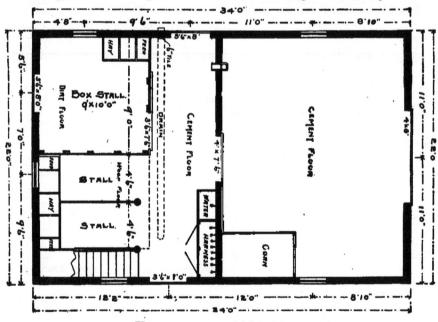

FIRST FLOOR BARN.

EAST END.

WEST END.

under the plank to give them the proper pitch. Another cross piece an inch thick is placed in the middle to strengthen the plank, back of this the planks have free ends which facilitate drainage back to the gutter and makes it easy to remove the floor if the planks should split or wear out.

The box stall may have an earth floor, if so desired, three or four inches thick, made of good stiff clay wet down and tamped level over the cement. Some horsemen prefer a cement bottom with a foot or two of straw; either way is good enough if the horses have the right kind of care.

The oat bin is in the hay loft and the corn bin may be put there too if the space on the carriage room floor is needed. By having the feed overhead and chutes for the different kinds of feed to the floor below, feeding is made easy.

Sliding doors usually are preferred for a horse barn, and a half door for ventilation

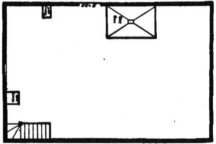

SECOND FLOOR.

is a good thing. A horse will stand for hours with his head out of such a door with evident satisfaction.

Serviceable Barn A172.

We are here illustrating a small barn, which is twenty feet by thirty-two feet, and contains a carriage room thirteen feet by nineteen feet, which has large double doors

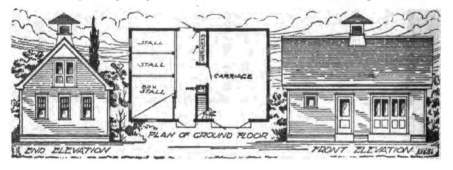

END ELEVATION   PLAN OF GROUND FLOOR   FRONT ELEVATION

in front that will admit the largest size carriage, a wide single door to the horse stable, and a stairway leading to the upper floor, which is for the storage of hay, feed, etc., and will admit the installation of a man's room if it is desired.

This barn contains two single stalls and a box stall. Each stall has a direct window, which is high enough from the floor to avoid too much draft on the horses and is protected by a wire mesh guard.

This barn has been designed for utility and is practical in every way. The arrangement is convenient, and it is of a neat appearance on the outside. If painted a stone gray, with all trimmings and cornice work painted pure white, it would be a credit to any neighborhood.

The carriage room has a cement floor, which is slightly pitched from all directions down to the center, where it is provided with a floor drain. This will admit the carriages to be washed any place in the room without injury to the floor and side walls, which are wainscoted with Portland cement

to a height of two feet six inches.

All the walls of the first story and ceiling are finished with clear southern yellow pine, beaded ceiling, with two coats of hard oil. This makes a very pretty effect for a stable and it is at the same time very serviceable. The stall floors are of double thickness one and three-quarter inch floors. The first floor is tongued and grooved, tightly laid, and then covered with hot tar. The upper floor is then laid and has slightly beveled edges, so that when laid the boards will fit tightly together at the bottom and leaving about an eighth of an inch crack on the top surface, which is then filled with hot tar. This construction makes a very durable and sanitary floor. The entire stall floor is pitched slightly to the rear to a cast iron gutter with perforated cover and connected with the catch basin and sewer. The second floor has ample storage room for a winter's supply of hay and feed for three horses and is of strong construction. The roof is of shingles and the ventilator gives the building a complete appearance.

Cement Rough-Cast Barn—A182.

A carriage house and stable plastered on the outside with cement mortar with a rough cast finish is shown in plan (A182). There are locations where a basement for laundry purpose under the house is not de-

ground and the sewers are not deep enough to permit much underground building so that basement laundries are not common. To meet just such conditions stables with laundry rooms just seem to fill the bill,

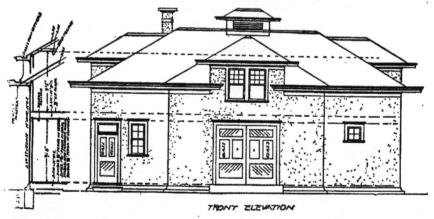

FRONT ELEVATION

sirable. This plan for a carriage house with a laundry attachment was designed especially to meet such cases. In New Orleans, La., such carriage houses are quite common. There is a great deal of made

especially when they are well designed and built to suit individual needs.

This building is substantial in appearance and the manner of construction is very satisfactory for a warm climate. The

BARN PLANS

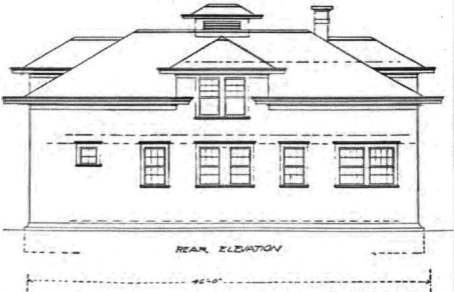

REAR ELEVATION

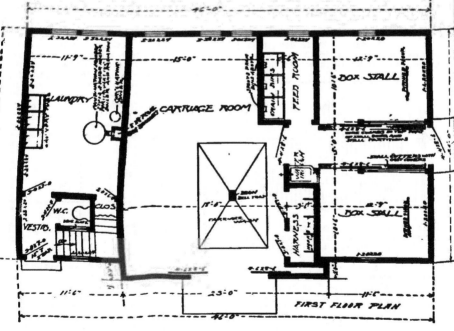

FIRST FLOOR PLAN

outside cement work when properly put on with metal lath is very durable. It looks well and it is not expensive.

The usual conveniences found in small barns are provided in this building, but it is a little more elaborate than ordinary. The box stalls are especially large and roomy, there is a larger feed room than is customary and the harness room is a little larger than we usually find in a small or medium sized stable. But the especial features about the building are the rooms for servants with an entrance separate from the carriage house and the laundry with its hot water heating apparatus, which not only furnishes hot water for washing and for stable use, but to warm the stable and the servants' rooms in winter. This laundry room is also large enough to hold the clotheslines in stormy weather, and there are plenty of windows for light.

Laundry work is a problem in the south as well as in the north. Those who get along with the least friction usually have the best possible conveniences for doing the work. Large light laundry rooms, supplied with plenty of hot water and furnished with good machinery and tubs that are rightly placed and fitted with the necessary faucets, waste pipes, etc., offer more inducements to do good work and less occasion for complaints than ordinary.

There are many advantages in having the laundry room away from the house. It avoids confusion in the house on wash days and the odors of dirty steam and soapy water are done away with.

For a pretentious property a stable building of this size and design looks well. The building is large enough to match up well with a good big residence, and the design and style of the roof shows character enough for a house, in fact many costly houses are built with roofs that are less attractive than this one. A carriage house like this is not complete without a good wide drive leading up to it. This design requires a smooth pavement in front of the building one-third wider than the building itself. It should have a pretentious approach to give it the proper setting. Sometimes an inferior building can be given a royal appearance by an elaborate entrance. A driveway to the stable is part of the entrance. In this plan the inside is right, the outside looks well and the driveway may easily be made to correspond.

Separate Horse Barn—A129.

A small, convenient horse barn, twenty-one by thirty-two feet in size, with considerable mow room is shown in this plan.

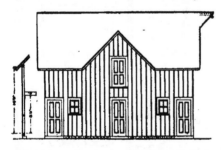

Such a barn is very convenient on some farms where for good reasons it is found best to keep horses in a building by themselves.

There are a good many farmers who object to stabling horses in the same building with other animals because they don't seem to mix just right. Horses are different in their habits from any other domestic animal and it seems right and proper to give them a building to themselves when possible. Besides, it often is more convenient to have a small horse barn near the house to save steps in doing the chores. A horse barn is in use every day in the year, while on many farms the cattle barns are not used much in summer. Then again a horse barn properly cared for

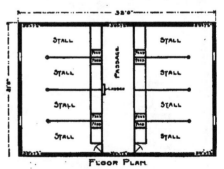

FLOOR PLAN.

has no disagreeable odor. It may be near the house without causing annoyance. Very often women have driving horses of their own and they like to look after them themselves to a certain extent, and they very much prefer to have them within easy reach. Also in case of fire there is a further advantage in having farm buildings separate.

The old English plan was to scatter farm buildings far enough apart to prevent a general conflagration in case one should take fire, but farm labor is less expensive in England and everybody knows that it costs more to care for animals housed in separate buildings because of the running back and forth and because you haven't a great big storage room all under one roof where feed may be hoisted by horse power and returned to the feeding floor by gravity.

In building a little horse barn like this it is better to put down good foundation walls reaching below frost. By making the passageway floor about three inches higher than the floor behind the horses an incline will be provided sufficient to keep the feed room floor dry as well as to give the neces-

sary drainage slope to the standing floor for the horses.

Most horsemen prefer to floor the horse stalls with planks, whether the bottom is cemented or not. This may be done before the partitions are put in, but it is better to plank each stall separately. In either case select planks two inches thick with tongue and groove matching and lay them with coal tar between. Give the floor a slight incline, say two inches fall in a distance of eight feet.

It is much better in a barn of this size, built for this purpose, to cover the whole bottom with a cement floor, cementing tight up against the walls all around and leaving a slight depression behind the horses; a sort of rounded open drain not more than an inch deep and slope the drain to the manure door so it is easy to wash the stalls and sweep the water out doors. A horse stable after this order will be found very convenient on any farm whether other buildings are calculated for horse stabling or not.

Cheap Horse Barn—A113.

A small barn with two double stalls and one single stall with standing room for another horse is offered in this plan. The barn is twenty-six feet wide and thirty-two feet long, one half of which is partitioned off for a stable and the other half

A barn that is open underneath makes a harbor for rats. It is better to have it

Noaru Side.

boarded up. The stable doors in this plan, both at the north side and the south side,

West End

is kept for carriage room and storage. There is no foundation under this barn except stone or brick corners and center supports, but it is a good plan to put a board around under the sill and bury the lower edge in the ground.

South Side.

East End

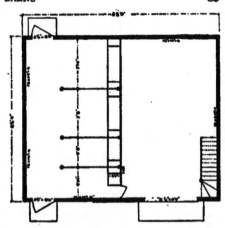

Floor Plan

are cut in two so the upper half may be opened for air and ventilation and the lower one remain shut to keep the animals from getting out and in. The plan is as simple as possible to make a barn and still have it look well. It is large enough to be of some use and it has quite a loft for hay. A cheap little barn like this answers the purpose as well as a more expensive one.

City Stable for Two Horses—A114.

A very neat carriage house is shown in plan (A114). It is intended to house two horses and have room enough for a couple

FRONT ELEVATION

of carriages. The building is supported by a stone wall three feet in the ground and one foot above ground to keep the floor well up, but the height, of course, must depend on the nature of the ground and location in reference to the street and driveway. It is not desirable to approach the main doorway by a very steep bridge because it is often necessary to run carriages out and in by hand. Of course, if it is necessary to set the floor up, the driveway may be raised accordingly, this, however, very often runs into considerable expense.

The way a driveway approaches the stable affects the appearance of the stable a good deal. Generally a pleasing effect may be obtained by a curved driveway where it it kept neatly trimmed at the sides. If the driveway is gently rounded and the edges kept about two inches lower than the sod, it is easy to maintain a clean track and a

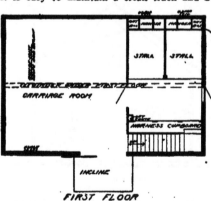

STALL STALL

CARRIAGE ROOM

HARNESS CUPBOARD

INCLINE

FIRST FLOOR

well defined edge without putting a whole lot of unnecesary work on it. The lawn mower will trim the grass and a spade used once a month will keep the edge of the drive in good shape.

The floor of this carriage house is made solid by running a heavy girder lengthwise of the building through the center. Joists are carried from the sills to meet on this

one and three-eighths matched hard pine.

In the stalls two inch planks are laid lengthwise, having an incline of two inches in the length of the stall. These planks are

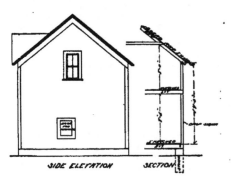

SIDE ELEVATION   SECTION

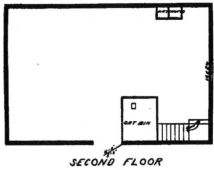

SECOND FLOOR

girder. The floor is double, the first layer being an inch thick dressed on one side, and to make the boards even in thickness is layed diagonally. On top of this is laid a layer of felt roofing topped with tar, both underneath and on top. The upper floor is

nailed to one cross piece in the middle and another cross piece a little thicker under the manger, but the nailing is not very solid because stable planks soon wear through and it is necessary to turn them end for end, sometimes within a year.

Small Livery Barn—A138.

For a village or small city this plan offers a comparatively cheap building that may be used to advantage by a man who keeps four or five horses for hire. Usually in such cases it is not necessary to have a great deal of feed storage room because the hay is baled and sometimes the straw comes in bales. A good harness room is necessary and it often happens that the hostler wants to sleep in the stable and this room, ten by fifteen feet, is sufficient for such purposes.

The problem in all livery stables is how to take care of the different rigs. There are cutters and sleighs to be taken care of

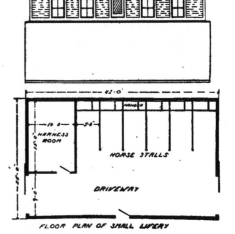

FLOOR PLAN OF SMALL LIVERY

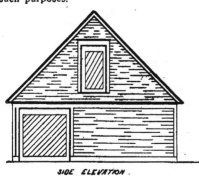

SIDE ELEVATION

nine or ten months in the year, when they are not in use, and there are wagons in the way almost all the time. Storage room is expensive and sometimes ground room is an object.

--Too often public stables are littered around outside of the building with old trash that should be sold for junk or burned up. Such conditions are more noticeable in the smaller places. But pride in keeping up one's property is just as valuable

and just as necessary in a village as in the city. Perhaps liverymen and blacksmiths are a little more careless in this respect than any other class of citizens. Why this should be so is a mystery. It costs nothing to be neat and neatness attracts trade in these lines as well as others. From general observation it would seem that a place for everything and everything in its place is a suggestion which applies to liverymen and blacksmiths all over the country.

Horse and Cow House—A131.

A small carriage house with stable room for two horses or a horse and a cow is a very convenient thing when a person has

pay for it. Of course a cow in a horse stall needs plenty of bedding, but where only one cow is kept it is easy enough to furnish all the litter necessary.

There are a good many designs for small

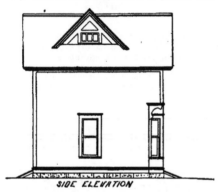

SIDE ELEVATION

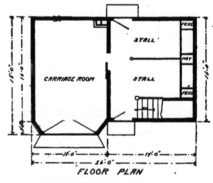

FLOOR PLAN

a good sized lot in the city or village. A horse stall makes a splendid stall for a cow, better than what is ordinarily designed for a cow stall because there is more room and it gives more comfort. A cow appreciates comfort and will give enough more milk to

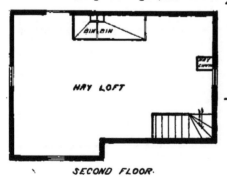

SECOND FLOOR.

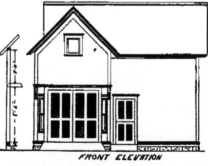

FRONT ELEVATION

carriage houses, some of which are decidedly homely. A good many of the fancy buildings are too expensive. Here is a comparatively cheap structure, but it is all right for looks and it is a convenient stable to do work in. There is a hay chute which reaches from the loft to the manger below with openings for both stalls, which is a very convenient arrangement and is worth a good deal just to keep the hay dust and chaff out of the horse's main and fore top. It also leaves the feed boxes in the corner of the mangers for grain and other feeds.

A carriage house like this may have a plank floor or the floor may be left out entirely and the ground leveled up with cinders except the stalls and the very best stall floor is made of stiff clay pounded in wet. Some of the most successful horsemen prefer a clay bottom stall.

Little Village Stable—A135.

The little barn, eighteen by twenty-four feet, as shown in the plans and elevations of (A135), is a convenient arrangement in either village or city. It is not expensive, in fact, it is probably as cheap as any satisfactory structure could be. It is better not to take up room in such a small barn in building a stairway, as the upright ladder placed against one of the partitions an-

sider it labor now, it is a part of their education and it is an important part too.

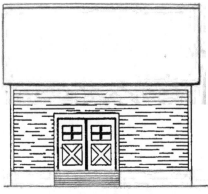

FRONT ELEVATION

Truth may be taught in a more thorough manner through mechanics than by any other means. The principle of learning a thing by doing it is just as valuable now as it was in Froebel's time.

SIDE ELEVATION

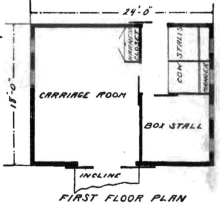

FIRST FLOOR PLAN

swers the purpose very well. To keep the cold from blowing down through the opening a light door with a pulley, cord and counter weight may be made to shut over the opening.

If there is a boy in the family he will find a way to rig up a work bench in the front corner of the carriage room between the door and the first window. It is easy to encourage boys to work with tools, especially since the graded schools have taken up manual training. The schools have added tone to the work, boys don't con-

DEPARTMENT OF

CATTLE SHEDS
AND
FEED LOTS

Feed Lots for Beef Cattle—A184—A184.

WHERE cattle are fed in large numbers it pays and pays well to fit up properly for the business. In the corn belt buying thrifty young cattle and finishing them for the market, is a splendid business in the hands of men who understand how to buy, how to feed and how to sell. The old fashioned way of putting a fence around a mudhole and confining a bunch of cattle in the mire for weeks or months at a time ceased to be profitable long ago, but unfortunately some men haven't found it out. Considerable engineering ability is required to plan and construct feed lots for the accommodation of large numbers of cattle in such a way as to make the animals comfortable and to economize labor.

Plan (A184) has received very careful attention in this respect. The storage barn and silos are set on a ridge of ground sloping preferably to the southwest. The feed lots thirty-two by seventy-two feet in size, including the shed, are fenced off one after another as many as needed. Two yards only are shown in the drawings because no matter how many you have each pair of two would be a repetition of this pair. The lots might be extended a quarter of a mile holding the same order.

It works better if the ground is about eight feet lower for the feed lots than it is for the storage barn and silos as this gives a chance to run the track from the floor of the storage barn over the heads of the cattle high enough to leave a passageway under for a pair of horses and a manure spreader. Eight feet in the clear is little enough and it is high enough because straw as well as feed will be brought to each lot by car on the overhead track.

The car is made large for this purpose, being four feet wide at the bottom, six feet wide at the top, four feet high and eight feet long with corner sockets for stakes to hold straw or hay. When filled with silage it will make quite a load, but one man can move it if the wheels are large and kept well oiled and if the track is level and true. Some feeding yards have an inclined track, but this is not necessary, in fact it is objectionable because the car will never stay where you want it and it is uphill work getting it back to be refilled. Make the track absolutely dead level and perfectly straight. Two by fours planted on top with two-inch band iron that has been hammered straight and true will answer very well but the two by fours must be well supported and thoroughly well spiked in place. In building the track remember that you are trying to save time and labor at every feeding period for a number of years to come. You want the track so true and the car wheels to fit so perfectly that the car will run along without much friction after getting it started.

One man with a rig like this that works right should feed a large bunch of cattle because he can take advantage of his work. In the first place he has got a car big enough to hold something. He runs a chute from the silo to the car which saves forking the silage up from the floor until the silo is nearly empty. The sides of the car are hinged so they drop down over the feeding racks in the yards. He loads the car quickly and easily and a good deal of the stuff unloads itself. The track is made in sixteen foot sections, as the yards are thirty-two feet wide the tracks have one support in the middle of the yard. The other supports form part of the fences between the yards.

In laying out the yards the problem of draining must be worked out first. It is impossible to have the yards dry unless ample provision is made for taking care of the rainfall. A drain tile is marked on the plan leading from the corner of the storage barn and running across the ends of the feeding pens down the whole length of the alley to an outlet in the field beyond. The brick pavement in each feed lot slopes to the center to lead the water to the tile drain underneath which connects with the trunk line of tile near the fence in the alley. This main drain increases in size to accommodate the extra drainage as it proceeds past the different pens.

An open shed twelve by thirty-two feet occupies one end of each yard. This shed is not paved but is kept well bedded. All the rest of the yard is paved with brick laid flat on a cinder bed.

An additional drain tile runs from each water tank to the trunk tile line to take care of any overflow from the tank. In some locations another tile drain will be necessary at the back of the shed to take care of the drip from the eaves because the ground must be kept dry.

Water Supply.

Good fresh water in sufficient quantity to supply the needs of the cattle in these feed lots is quite a problem in itself. The water must be good and there must be plenty of it. To save labor it must also be supplied under pressure and carried to each water tank in pipes placed underground below

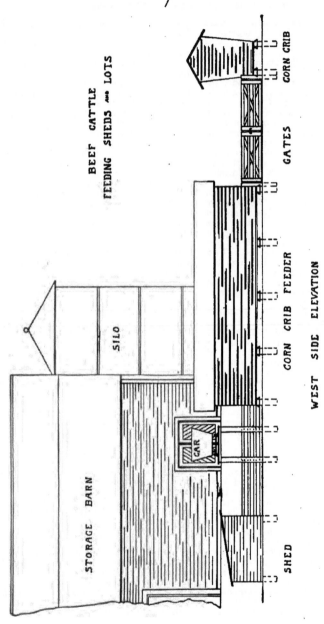

BEEF CATTLE
FEEDING SHEDS AND LOTS

WEST SIDE ELEVATION

frost. There must be a valve placed in each pipe running to each water tank so constructed that it won't freeze. The stems from these valves should be extended up to the overhead track so a man can walk from one end of the feeding yards to the other and regulate the water easily and quickly.

Generally the water must be supplied by a windmill and a reservoir of some kind. A cement basin in a nearby hillside and protected from frost is perhaps the most satisfactory because when once made it is permanent. The source must be sufficient to supply it and the windmill or other power which does the pumping must be powerful enough to do the work at all times. .You cannot afford to take chances on a water famine with several hundred feeding cattle on your hands.

Storage Barn.

In the plan not much attention is paid to the storage barn except that it shows the most convenient location. Every feeder must plan storage to suit his way of doing business. If he has a large farm on which he grows alfalfa, grain and other crops that make large quantities of roughage he must provide an extensive storage barn with appliances to get the stuff in and to get it out again when needed for feeding.

Generally speaking, the barn should be large and high. The capacity of a storage barn is increased by additional height at a very rapid ratio because all kinds of loose fodder packs very close in the bottom and lies very loose at the top. A deep bay may be filled to the peak with hay at haying time and settle sufficiently to hold a large quantity of sheaf-wheat a few weeks later, but a shallow mow don't hold much at any time. It don't have the weight sufficient to pack it.

There will, of course, be a good solid floor over the car track and there will be chutes or openings to let the hay down directly into the car and there will be ladders in the chutes to let a man down into the car to tramp it full. The same horse fork that is used to put the fodder in will move the stuff from the other parts of the barn to this floor as it is needed.

Brick Pavement.

There is only one way to have a feeding lot clean and that is to pave it. There are different kinds of pavements more or less virtuous but the cheapest satisfactory bottom for a feeding yard is brick laid on a foundation of sand and cinders. The cinders help drainage and prevent the bricks

heaving with the frost. It is easier to lay the bricks level and smooth if an inch or two of sharp sand is scattered over the top of the cinders. The sand holds the bricks in place and a little sand does not prevent the water from getting away.

A great deal depends on the foundation. The ground should be graded with the proper slope to the center gutter. It is not necessary to have an opening in the bricks, the cracks between the bricks are sufficient, but a line of tile should be carefully laid underneath deep enough to be out of the way of frost. Frost does not penetrate deep in a feeding yard under a brick pavement. During some winters the ground won't freeze. There is more or less litter scattered about that prevents hard freezing. Probably if the tile starts a foot below the brick at the shed end and deepens to two and one-half feet where it joins the trunk tile in the alley the drain will give no trouble.

Lay the tile first smoothly and evenly and cover the joints with pieces of broken tile, then fill in with coarse cinders using no earth over the tile. Tile in a mud-bottom yard seldom works satisfactorily because the tramping of the cattle packs the mud so that the water can't get through. A mud-bottom yard has never been drained and the chances are that such a yard never will be drained in a satisfactory manner.

Commence laying the brick in the center over the tile and work both ways to the fences. The herring bone style of laying brick gives the best satisfaction. No two brick tip alike when laid like this. Of course you want every brick to lay flat and level, but you don't always get just what you want. If good hard burned bricks are laid flat, herring bone style on a good foundation you will have more comfort and satisfaction than you ever had in a feeding lot before. If you have lots of money to use and don't care for expense then put in a cement pavement and build it just the same as sidewalks are built. You will then have a yard that will last a life-time, but it won't be as dry as the brick because the water must all run to the end or center outlet on top of the pavement before it can get away.

The Shed.

A continuous shed is designed to run the whole length of the feeding plant without a break. The shed is twelve feet wide and eight feet high in front and six feet six inches high at the back. The shed faces the south and the front is left open to admit sunshine. The construction is light and

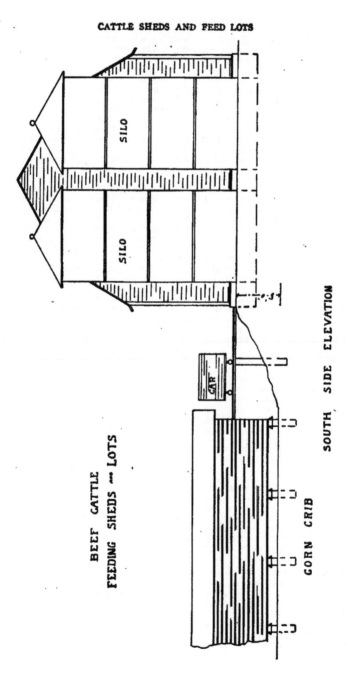

BEEF CATTLE
FEEDING SHEDS AND LOTS

SOUTH SIDE ELEVATION

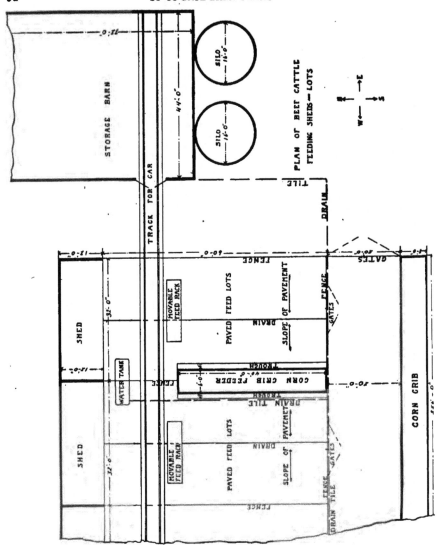

cheap as shown in the detail drawing. There are no partitions except the fences between pens which run to the back of the shed, in fact the fence posts and shed posts are the same.

Two by six rafters fourteen feet long are used for the roof. These are covered with sheathing boards, dressed one side, and on this is stretched a good quality of felt roofing. The north side is banked with cinders to prevent the cold winds from blowing under and the ground floor of the shed slopes to the brick pavement. A liberal supply of straw for bedding is kept in the shed and this is carefully shaken up and the dung picked out every day.

Feeders now-a-days appreciate the importance of making animals comfortable. It takes a good deal of feed to supply the heat dissipated by animals lying on the cold ground. Straw is cheaper than corn.

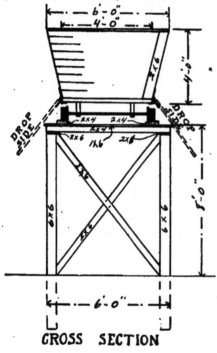

CROSS SECTION
OF CAR

Beef cattle don't require much protection against the cold. Their thick winter hair and hides are sufficient if they are kept dry and well fed. Cattle will gain a little faster on the same amount of feed if kept warmly stabled, but they must have fresh air and extra expense of individual attention when handling them in a stable more than eats up the additional profits from the extra gains made. A feeding rack well up above the ground along the back of the shed is a good thing at times in rainy weather; it induces the cattle to stay inside. It is better to put the feeding racks on the ground when you use them regularly every day, but ground space in the shed is limited and such racks will be used occasionally only.

For this reason it is not desirable to take up any more ground space than necessary for this purpose.

Corn Crib.

On the south side of the alley way is a corn crib six feet wide at the bottom, eight feet wide at the top, ten feet high above the foundation posts and as long as necessary. This crib is intended for storage purposes to hold corn enough to last all winter. There is a door in the end and doors along the alley side sixty-four feet apart, each door being opposite the door of a feeder crib. A temporary bridge reaches from one door to the other so the carrying may be done with a wheelbarrow or car running on a track. As the bridge is intended to be moved from one feeder crib to the next a wheelbarrow would be handier than a car because it is lighter and may be easily moved.

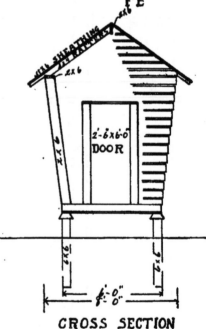

CROSS SECTION
OF CORN CRIB

Feeder Cribs.

Between each pair of feeding pens is a feeder crib six feet wide at the bottom, eight feet wide at the top and eight feet high. These cribs are forty feet long extending back from the alley fence. This gives forty lineal feet of corn trough for each feeding yard. These feeding troughs are made by extending the two by four floor across joists two feet beyond the sills at each side. The floor in the crib is laid on top of these cross joints and the feeder boxes are made by boarding on the under side and across the ends. This makes the floor of the feeder trough about five inches lower than the floor of the crib which permits the corn to work out easily and in case of a driving storm the water does not run in from the feed troughs to wet the crib floor.

Some little experimenting is necessary to get the opening the right size. A smaller opening answers when the trough is lower than the corn floor. A narrow strip may be nailed in the opening at the top if it is found too large.

The roofs of these feeder cribs are made by using sixteen foot boards full length. The projection keeps the feeder troughs dry and provides a little shelter for the animals when feeding. For the comfort of the cattle it is a good plan to run eave troughs the whole length of these roofs.

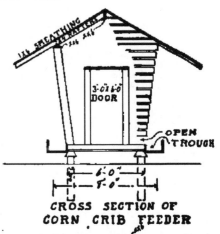

CROSS SECTION OF CORN CRIB FEEDER

would be housed in the main storage crib.

It is not every feeder of beef cattle who approves of self feeder cribs, but if they don't like to have the animals help themselves the same cribs and the same troughs

DETAIL OF BRICK PAVEMENT

The water could be carried to the water tanks or the drain in the alley.

At corn harvest time these feeder cribs of course would be filled first with the earliest and best seasoned corn to feed first. The later and poorer quality of corn

CROSS SECTION OF SHED

will be just as useful, so that the man who really loves to work may dig the corn out, load it in a basket and carry it around to the side of the crib and distribute it along the troughs. It will pay some men to do this, men who are built that way. Each man must work in his own harness.

Silos.

For some unaccountable reason beef men have entertained a prejudice against silos. But not every man who feeds cattle without their assistance objects to silos. In many cases they have more corn stalks than they can feed without trying to save the last vestige of the corn crop and they think the animals can cut the feed and mow it away cheaper than it can be done by machinery, but the fact remains that nearly one-half of the feeding value of the corn crop is in the stalks and leaves of the corn plant. If cut just at the right time, when the sap is all in the stalk, then cut up fine and packed away in an airtight silo the stalks lose very little of their feeding value. They may be kept a year and the last silage from the bottom comes out as fresh and apparently as palatable as the first. Cattle will even leave pasture in the summer time to eat left over silage. If we ask the animals what they think of it their actions are strongly in the affirmative. We must study these things in detail to thoroughly understand our business.

Looking at the silo problem from the broadest side it certainly would pay to put some of the crop in silos. The stalks from eight or ten acres will fill a sixteen by thirty-two foot silo so that most feeders would only have an opportunity to cut off one side of the corn crop and they would still have a large quantity of stalks to go to waste.

The silos in the plan are made of two by eight pine planks dressed both sides, the edges beveled and put together like a tub. They are hooped with three-quarter inch round iron hoops drawn up with nuts against the shoulders of cast-iron plates as shown in the detail drawing on another page.

This feeding plant is designed to save labor and to utilize feed to the best possible advantage. It would be difficult to build a large plant any cheaper and have it satisfactory. It would also be difficult to build, on any other plan, a thoroughly practical plant that could be extended indefinitely as the business grows without altering or rebuilding.

Hollow Square Cattle Shed—A155.

Sheds on three sides of a hollow square is an old style way of building feeding sheds. It is probably the best way now

the whole length of the shed. The hollow square proposition has the advantage of warmth because it is protected from the

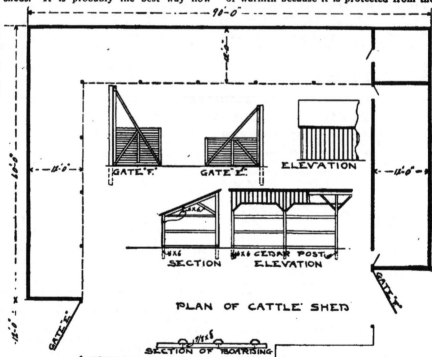

except that it is more difficult to economize labor with this construction than it is with a straight away proposition where you can run a railway and a feed truck

east, west and north winds. Yards like this are always built opening towards the south.

In this plan there are convenient gates

to drive in when bringing roughage or other feed to the cattle. The gates to look well should be made right and left and they should have automatic device to fasten them quickly. Animals confined in a yard in the winter time are crazy to get out. They learn how to slip alongside of a wagon and crowd through the gate when the driver is engaged with his team. This is a source of annoyance that can hardly be avoided, but good gates that swing easily and fasten quickly help a good deal.

Straight Away Cattle Shed—A123.

Some kind of a cattle shed is necessary in connection with every feed lot. Plan (A123) shows a cheap cattle shed ninety feet long and ten feet six inches wide. It is built of two by fours for framing, covered with boards twelve feet and sixteen feet long which cut to advantage without waste except at the ends.

There is a low-down manger which runs

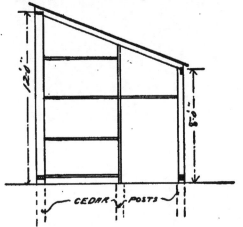

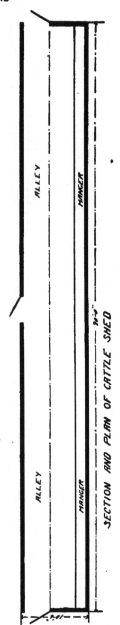

SECTION AND PLAN OF CATTLE SHED

the full length of the shed against the back wall. The front side of the manger is bedded in the ground which, together with a little banking on the outside, prevents the cold winds from blowing under. Some feeders fail to realize the importance of this precaution. The north wind seems much colder when it forces through a small opening. There is something about the bottom of the north side of a cattle shed that seems to invite a current of air from the north, but this feed manger arrangement seems to get the better of it. Mangers should be low for another reason. For thousands of years cattle have been accustomed to feed from the ground. While in the pasture they keep their heads down nearly all the time, but for some unaccountable reason they are expected to hold their heads two or three feet high when being fed artificially.

DEPARTMENT OF

POULTRY HOUSES

Building Poultry Houses

THERE are a few general principles which apply to all poultry houses. In the first place the location must be dry and it should be sheltered from the cold winds, not by placing the house at the foot of a hill, but by tree-belts, high tight board fences, or buildings. Remember that cold air settles in low places. A low place though sheltered from wind storms is often more disagreeable to poultry than a bleak hill-top. Cold air slides down hill because it is heavier than warm air.

In regard to exposure a south frontage is the best, next to south front the house southeast or east. Chickens prefer morning sun to afternoon sun. They are early birds and want to see the first reflection of daylight.

On general principles a convenient poultry house is to be desired because it saves work at feeding time. On the other hand, the colony house plan saves work by giving the fowls an opportunity to feed themselves to a certain extent. It is easy to figure how many steps are saved in the course of a week or a year by having the fowls carefully housed all under one roof, but it is not so easy to estimate the amount of feed that poultry will pick up in an orchard where the colony houses are separated by distances ranging from twenty feet to a hundred yards according to circumstances.

It is plain that no one plan offers all the advantages and it is equally patent that no other plan embraces all the objectionable features.

A building with a shed roof requires a little more material than a building the same size with a double roof because the roofing material in both instances is practically the same and the drop in the double roof takes off just so much of the siding.

To offset this, however, is the advantage of getting more sunshine into a house with a shed roof. To economize warmth in winter it is a good plan to have the back of the house as low as possible. Some even build down to three feet. Unless the roof is quite steep this manner of building leads to a good deal of stooping on the part of the attendant. If the roof is steep there is no material or space saved. Alley ways in poultry houses take up considerable room, but they also furnish storage for feed and implements.

The subject of ventilation has bothered poultry men more than any other one thing. It is extremely difficult to get up a circulation of air in a poultry house and you cannot have ventilation without circulation. Some poultry men claim to have solved the problem by leaving out all ventilating shafts and covering the openings with comparatively thin cotton, others leave the gable windows open and fill the roof space with straw.

Sunlight is necessary to fowls. It prevents diseases, and encourages cheerfulness. Fowls basking in the sun usually are contented and happy, but fowls cannot stand too much sun in hot weather. There must be partial shade in summer.

A poultry house is not complete without a yard. Nine times out of ten the yard is too small, partly because large yards are not appreciated and partly because poultry fencing is expensive.

In these plans we are showing up the different kinds of houses so that individual farmers may select a plan that just suits their location and the way in which they prefer to conduct the poultry branch of their business.

Small Double Poultry House—A151

A poultry house with an open scratching shed. The house is thirty-four feet long by twelve in width. Poultry men differ about the width of a house constructed in

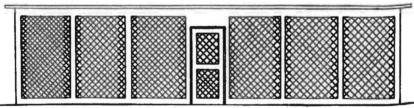

ELEVATION

this manner. Some prefer twelve feet because it is easier to get the sunlight clear to the back, as these houses should always front the south. On the other hand men with considerable experience prefer houses sixteen or even twenty feet in width because thy can house more fowls for practically the same amount of money.

There are many ways of building an open scratching shed and poultry house, but this plan seems to contain about everything that is necessary. The door opening into the hen-house is just a frame covered with cotton which admits both light and air to the roosts and nest boxes. The outside

and have white frost on the inside when all the stables on the farm are comparatively dry has bothered more men than anything else in the poultry line. It is easier to build a satisfactory stable for any other domestic animal than it is for chickens unless we are satisfied with what is commonly termed a curtain front house. The phrase curtain front simply means that some of the openings are covered with thin cotton instead of glass. It seems to have solved the problem of how to make a chicken house light, airy and dry, but not all curtain front houses work alike. A great deal depends on the head room. A few

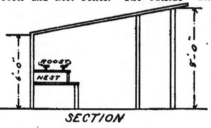

SECTION

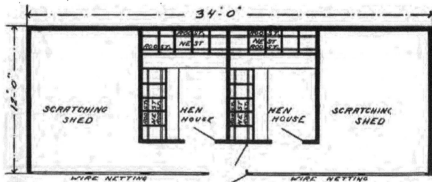

FLOOR PLAN OF CHICKEN HOUSE

wire netting may be covered with cotton or not according to the climate and the ideas of the owner.

The roofing is tarred paper and it starts at the highest point in front, turns over the upper corner at the back and goes clear down to the ground. This makes a thoroughly wind proof and damp proof house.

It is a peculiar thing about the dampness in poultry houses. It is a comparatively simple question that has bothered poultry men more than anything else. Why a poultry house should gather dampness

hens have not body warmth enough to heat a great deal of space. You cannot have good ventilation without heat. The solution seems to be to build a comparatively small house with a low roof. Some poultry men build their curtain front houses as low as two feet at the back and only about six or seven feet high in the front.

But this makes a back-aching job in taking care of the fowls unless the attendant is built on the "shorty" plan. Hens require little head room. Most poultry houses are built to accommodate the attendant to the detriment of the hens.

Another Small Double Poultry House—A 154

A small double poultry house. It is twenty-four feet long and sixteen feet wide, giving a space of sixteen by twelve feet to each compartment. It is very simple and it is also cheap and durable. It may be built of matched stuff with the smooth side turned in, or it may be constructed of rough lumber. Of course

in front, carried over the peak and clear down to the ground at the back.

Inside, the house is practically all one room, but a roost curtain may be hung with a roller to pull down at night or the cotton may be tacked on a hinged frame to let down at night, also one or more of the windows may be left open and the spaces covered with cotton.

POULTRY HOUSE

matched stuff is very much the best as it leaves no harbor for vermin and no lodgement for dust. In either case the building is covered outside with tarred paper. The paper is started, in strips, from the eaves

Against the back wall is the droppings board with the roosts above it and the nest boxes underneath. All this furnishing is made removable so far as possible for easy cleaning. The apron board in front of the nest boxes lifts out in sections.

Open Front Poultry House—A110

The modification of the popular open front poultry house. It is suitable for two lots of hens of forty or fifty each, accord-

at the back. No room is taken up in hallways or passageways but the doors entering the warm rooms open from the scratching sheds.

Very light material is used in the construction of this house. Sills are four by

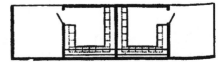

ing to the size of the breed. The house is forty feet long and ten feet wide, divided into two compartments. Each compartment has a warm room and a scratching shed which is open to the south. This makes each room ten feet square with a roof eight feet high in front and four feet

six inches, and two by fours are used for rafters. Common lumber is used for boarding, which is covered on the outside with building paper and the building paper is

covered with thin matched sheathing. For the roof common sheathing boards are laid close together and covered with tarred paper and the paper covered with shingles.

This makes a warm roof which is very essential in a poultry house.

Each of the closed pens has a window that reaches down to the sill. This window is wide enough and high enough to let in a great deal of sunshine, and this is what the chickens need in winter. All inside surfaces are dressed to prevent lodgement of dust and hiding places for vermin. The whole bottom of the building is filled in several inches deep with grout mortar. In the warm rooms the floor joists are embedded in the soft mortar and a matched floor laid on. A floor like this is dry and easily cleaned and it is impossible for rats to work their way up through it. There is no wooden floor in the scratching sheds. The grout filling is supposed to be covered with straw a foot or so in depth. The hens will work in this straw even in the coldest days, but of course it is a good plan to have a liberal supply of straw in the warm room for amusement night and morning.

For nest boxes the arrangement given in this plan is very satisfactory. It shows a roosting platform with a row of nests underneath. For leghorns or similar fowls twelve inches square and ten or eleven inches high is large enough for the nest boxes, but for brahmas or cochins two or three inches larger each way is much better. To facilitate cleaning, the dropping board and nest boxes lift off from the lower platform. The lower platform is hinged and may be dropped down or unhooked and the whole thing carried outdoors. It is very important to have roosting poles, dropping board and nest boxes loose. A great deal of trouble has come from vermin getting into these places without having facilities to eradicate them easily.

Hens seldom form the egg eating habit if the nests are dark. This is why the boxes open from the back under cover. The dropping board is not fastened to the next boxes in any way. When gathering the eggs it may be lifted easily.

Community House—A199.

A modification of the colony house is what is called by some poultry men a community house. It is larger than the colony house, too large in fact to move about conveniently, but a system of community houses may be built in the orchard and connected with wire netting to form yards for winter use. The netting may be removed in the spring for cultivation and the fowls permitted to forage about the orchard during the summer. A convenient way to do this is to cut poultry netting in proper lengths, fasten each end to good solid uprights and fasten the uprights to the houses with good strong wire loops which hold the posts both top and bottom. A lever is necessary to spring the posts into the loops in order to have the wire tight enough. Light stakes may then be driven at intervals and the netting fastened to the stakes with wire or twine.

The interior furnishings in these community houses are very simple. They con-

ROOST
NESTS
SECTION   ELEVATION

sist of movable nest boxes, movable dusting boxes and movable roost poles placed over movable droppings-boards.

In building these houses it is a good plan to make the floors double with paper between. Then block the houses up high enough to admit cats and dogs to clean out the rats when they become troublesome. Use plenty of good building paper and make the houses tight, leaving no cracks for drafts and no openings except a window and door and a small exit for the fowls into the yard.

The size of these houses is eight feet by twelve, seven feet high in front and five feet high in the rear. They may be blocked up on stone or short posts set in the ground three on a side, and one in the middle. Such houses will accommodate about twenty layers or forty brooder chicks. There is a great advantage in having the yards - between the houses as it leaves the front open so the attendant has easy access to any house without going through other houses or yards.

Double Brooder and Chicken House.

Plan A 202 shows an economical brooder house. The house accommodates 130 or 140 chicks, taking them from the incubator of the house. It makes a house large enough for poultry to work in during bad weather when the birds must be kept in-

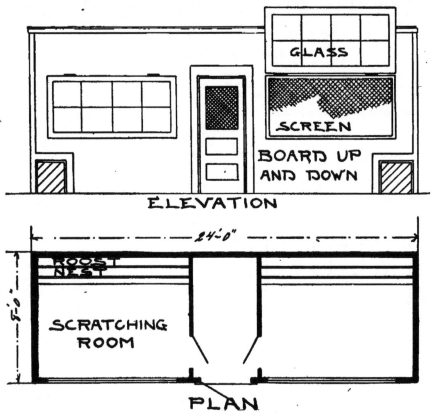

and housing them until they go into the regular poultry quarters.

This house is twelve feet long, seven feet wide, six feet high in front and four feet high at the back which allows standing room for a short man in the front part

doors and there is room for the attendant to move about when caring for the brood.

The house is placed on shoes two by six inches, placed flatways and rounded like sled runners. These runners are fourteen feet long which extends them a foot outside beyond each end of the building. An auger hole is bored through each end of each runner so a chain may be attached for pulling the house to another place.

The floor is made of two thicknesses of ⅞ inch stuff, dressed one side, breaking joints to prevent air currents. The walls and roof are covered with roofing paper. There is a window each side of the door hinged at the top and there is a wire screen on the inside of each window also hinged at the top to swing in and fasten up against the wall with a button. Windows hinged in this way are liked by poultry men generally better than sliding windows for two reasons: they can be made longer and when partly open will admit the fresh air and keep out the rain and snow.

There are low temporary partitions inside to divide the building in two parts, and a brooder is placed in each compartment. The brooders are blocked up from the floor slightly and set a little away from the sides of the building which is necessary to secure warmth and sufficient circulation. Inclines are used to make easy access to the brooders for the small chicks, but the inclines may be dispensed with later as the chickens grow. In the warm season the windows are turned to the north and in cold weather to the south. By keeping the runners blocked up from the ground a house built like this lasts a long time.

Farm Poultry House—A200.

A very neat farm poultry house is shown in this plan. The house is sixteen feet in width and twenty-four feet long, and eight

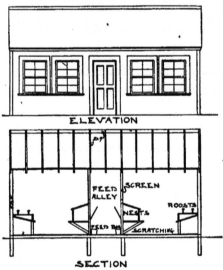

ELEVATION

SECTION

feet high to the eaves, with a hallway in the center four feet wide, leaving each poultry room ten by sixteen feet. Droppings boards extend along the outer sides the full width of the building and they are high enough up to leave scratching room underneath. The roosts are all on a level above the droppings boards. Rows of nest boxes extend along the partitions so the eggs may be gathered without going in amongst the hens. Feeding troughs also set along the floor in the feed alley so the hens can reach through for feed and water. The back end of the alley is used for storage purposes. A concrete foundation makes it rat proof and the concrete is covered about a foot deep with earth and the earth is supposed to be covered about a foot deep at all times with straw.

Both inside partitions are wire and there are wire doors in these partitions opening into the different departments. Loose strips reach across from one plate to another and the space above these strips is filled with straw to facilitate ventilation without draft, which is helped by windows

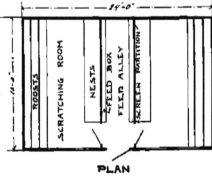

PLAN

in each gable end covered with very thin cotton. Twice during the winter season these strips are pulled down, the straw all taken out and fresh straw put in. This, of course, is done on a mild day when the fowls can be left out in the yard long enough to clean and disinfect the house thoroughly.

Portable Poultry House.

In some sections small portable houses, on wheels, are used for the young fry to house them all summer. The little houses are hauled away to different parts of pas- hens a row of nests is rigged up extending along one side. Such little houses are not suitable for full grown hens as a general thing because they would not accommodate

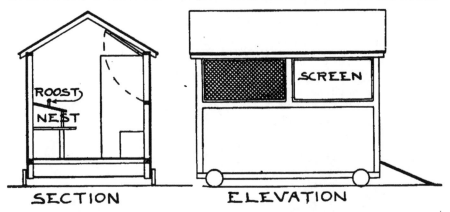

SECTION　　　ELEVATION

ture lots and meadows and the chickens permitted to run out. The style shown in No. A 201 is supported on small, wide wooden wheels driven on the ends of a rod which extends from one side of the house to the other.

When necessary to use such houses for more than a dozen, and this would hardly pay. However, there are circumstances under which such houses may be valuable even for laying hens. They may be built with or without a floor, or the floor may be simply loose boards to be put in and taken out as wanted.

Colony House—A198.

Some poultry raisers make good use of colony houses. It is a plan that works in

ELEVATION

well where land is plentiful and especially where fruit is grown extensively. They are small enough to move from one part of the orchard to another.

Experience goes to show that these houses may be placed from one hundred to two hundred yards apart without the different flocks mixing to any great extent. Poultry has been housed for so many generations that they have become attached to their roosting place and will not as a usual thing stray very far away. It is a very economical way of keeping poultry in the summer time because they pick up nearly all their living and they eat things that fruit men are very anxious to get rid of, such as wormy or diseased fruit and large quantities of injurious insects. Another great advantage is that the houses may be made very cheap.

The one shown in the cut is eight feet square on the ground. The only frame work is four short corner posts two feet long each and the boards are nailed on these forming a box, either with or without a floor. If a floor is used it will be necessary to use two by fours along the sides, at the bottom and these may be made to extend slightly beyond the ends of the building to use for runners when the house is moved. The roof is made of boards running up and down which may be either battoned or shingled. Shingles, of course, are the best and make the most permanent roof. No windows are used, the three openings in the front end are covered with cotton as shown. Colony houses are not to be recommended for the winter. It costs too much labor to attend to the fowls.

Hexagonal Poultry House—A174.

The house shown is in the shape of a hexagon and makes a very handsome and convenient house, and is just the thing for the city lot, where space is limited. The ground or floor plan will show the interior arrangement. The size of this house is ten feet six inches, and each of the six sides is

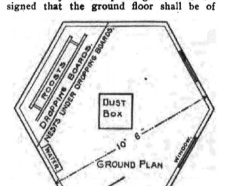

ELEVATION.

In nearly all the plans given it is designed that the ground floor shall be of

six feet in length. The corner posts are six feet long and the center of the house nine feet from floor to peak of roof. The house should be built with one window facing directly south and the other facing southeast, thus allowing an abundance of sunlight to enter the building in the morning when it is most needed.

earth, which is, in most cases, the most satisfactory floor material, and should be used whenever practical. Cement floors are also good, where they are used the poultry house will generally present a more attractive appearance and can be kept cleaner, with less labor, than a house having earth or wooden floors.

Practical Poultry House—A168

A single section of a two-pen poultry house fourteen by twenty-four feet is given in this plan. The house, of course, may be any length by adding any number of twen-

PERSPECTIVE VIEW

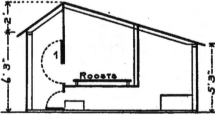

ty-four foot sections. It is placed so that the windows look to the south to gather all the sunlight possible.

A passageway on the north side, where the roof is high to make head room, is partitioned off and the work of feeding is done along this passage. A door lifts up in front of the roosts from this passageway to facilitate cleaning. It is not necessary to enter the scratching room very often because most of the attention may be given from the alley way. With the exception of the space occupied by the dust boxes the whole floor, except this passageway, is given over to scratching purposes as the roosts and dropping boards are elevated so the chickens can work under them. A section of this house will accommodate from twenty to thirty birds according to the size.

Poultry men will argue by the hour about the necessity of an alley way. There are many different opinions. Some think an alley is worth all the room it takes up just to prevent annoying the fowls when feeding by going in and out from amongst

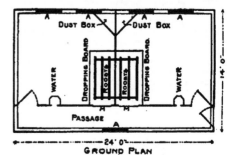

GROUND PLAN

them. Other poultry men think that chickens ought to be tame enough to pay very little attention to the feeder when he goes about his work, but it is generally noticeable that a hen makes quite a fuss when she

thinks she is about to be cornered. This applies to hens that are ordinarily tame as well as those that are ordinarily wild.

Inexpensive Poultry House—A170

This cheap little poultry house is ten feet square on the ground, the front is eight feet and the rear five feet high. Where only from ten to twelve hens are kept this

PERSPECTIVE VIEW

two by four for the door and window frames. The window frame consists of a two by four at the bottom and another two by four at the top, spaced to hold the

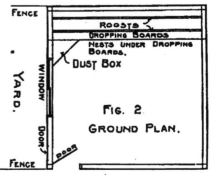

FIG. 2. GROUND PLAN.

little house will be found very useful. The only openings are a door in the east side, the large window on the south side and the little door to permit poultry to pass in and out.

A little house like this can be built if so desired without so much as a frame, except two by fours at the top and bottom to nail the boards to and another piece of

sashes in such a way as to permit them to pass back to leave the opening free. It is a good plan to have a wire netting over the window outside and a muslin curtain inside. A curtain may roll up on a window shade roller, so that it may be pulled down over the opening on cold days and rolled up when the sun shines warm. Such a curtain should be thin enough to let the air through freely. It is a splendid ventilator for a poultry house because it lets the air in and out gently without any draft. Some poultry houses are built without glass, thin muslin being depended on for both light and air. Such houses are usually dry and it is well known that a poultry house must be dry or the fowls won't do well.

A poultry house like this must have a good floor. One of the greatest annoyances in poultry keeping is to have rats burrow underneath. Rats prefer a poultry house to any other building because

there is always feed around that they can get and there is always water. Rats li e eggs, too, and they have been known to sample young chickens, but it is easy to block them out of a poultry house by mak ing a concrete floor. Concrete for this purpose may be pretty much all sand and gravel. Most any kind of a composition will answer the purpose. A little lime and a little cement, or lime without cement, or cement without lime mixed up with water in most any proportion will do the business. It should be pounded in and come up about even with the sill.

Small Chicken House—A119.

A very neat little chicken house. In size it is only 7x16 feet, but it makes comfortable quarters for 15 or 20 hens. It is set

ing. The roosts also are loose and may be removed easily.

This is just the kind of a house to start

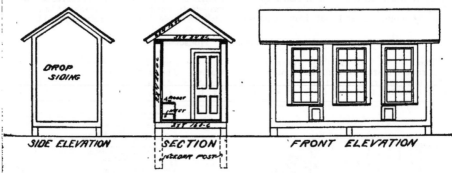

SIDE ELEVATION   SECTION   FRONT ELEVATION

on posts a foot or two from the ground to be out of the way of rats.

The floor is made warm by having it double boarded with a thickness of building paper between. The large windows of course face the south and the dust boxes are placed immediately in front of them because that is the way biddy likes to take a dust bath. She wants it directly in the sunlight if possible.

It is not necessary or desirable to go into a little house like this very often. It is so small that the presence of an attendant frightens the hens and causes a disagreeable commotion. By proper management, however, they can usually be let out into the yard when the presence of an attendant in the house becomes necessary. The roosts are placed over the nest boxes and the entrance to the nest boxes is in the rear. The nest box cover, which also is the dropping board, is loose and may be easily taken out through the door for clean

a boy in the poultry business. Boys take more interest in a small poultry house than they do in a house full size.

A little house like this is helped out very much by having a good yard in which considerable green stuff may be grown for

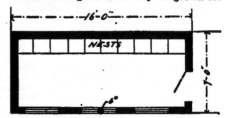

the fowls to pick at. By planting a little grain and a variety of vegetables, the poultry will pick up a good deal of feed and the fowls will be more healthy because of it.

An A-Shaped Poultry House—A152.

An A-shaped poultry house. This is the cheapest way to build a poultry house. You don't have to build a roof, or if you build a roof you don't have to build sides. You can do either way you choose.

the ridge pole and made flush on the curtain side. You attach the roller to the ridge pole so the curtain rolls up on the inside of the roller which brings it close to the woodwork.

The house shown in the plan is eight

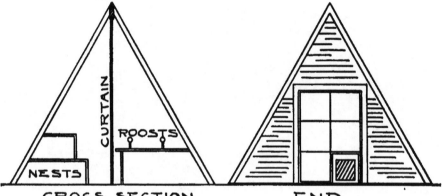

CROSS SECTION   END

It is divided lengthwise with a curtain partition. This curtain is in four foot sections and it rolls up on heavy window shade rollers, so that it may be pulled down

feet wide and sixteen feet long. One end of this building is supposed to front the south. There is a small door in this end for the chickens to go in and out and the

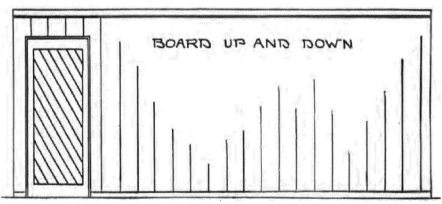

SIDE

cold nights to make a warm roosting place. The material of the curtain is cheap cotton, costing three or four cents per yard. The sections are divided by two by four posts reaching from the floor to

window is as big as possible. The entrance door is at the side and it should be near the south end. It is a bad plan to have doors, windows or any openings in the north end or north side of a poultry house.

DEPARTMENT OF

MISCELLANEOUS

PLANS

Building Ice-Houses and Storing Ice.

IT is easy to keep ice all summer if you know how. When ice is stored away for summer use and leaks away before it is wanted there is a reason for it. In the first place there must be a sufficient quantity of ice together to keep cold, and there must be protection against warm air and there must be no leak in the roof.

Some of the first farmer ice-houses were built underground or partly so. It often happened that drainage was imperfect and that water accumulated in and around the bottom of the house and melted the ice so that by the middle of summer, sometimes even before the month of June, the ice would all be gone.

Years ago it was considered necessary to make very expensive walls to keep the ice from melting and a great many experiments have been conducted for the purpose of finding out the best way to build ice-houses. The right principle of refrigerator building has confused builders of ice-houses, and some of them have not yet recognized the difference.

An ice-house is intended to preserve ice while a refrigerator is intended to make use of it, economically of course, but when a piece of ice is put into a refrigerator it has a mission to perform. It is required to take the heat out of other material to preserve food products and it must dissipate itself in the process, while ice is placed in the ice-house to stay, to be preserved until wanted for use.

An open shed will preserve ice, or it may be piled up in a field and kept all summer by simply putting a cover over it to keep off the rain and an inner cover of saw-dust to keep out the air. Such a crude way of keeping ice is necessarily wasteful, but not to the extent popularly supposed.

It is quite possible to put a cube of ice twelve feet through in a cheaply constructed building and so pack it with saw-duct as to keep it in a very satisfactory way until wanted during the summer months. The roof must be tight because water dropping often in the same spot will bore a hole through the saw-dust covering down to the ice; warm air will follow and we all know that air must be kept away from ice or it will melt rapidly.

Drainage is another very important consideration. The bottom must be air-tight, but it must be porous enough to allow water to percolate through. For this reason a bottom of rough stones covered with cinders and the cinders covered with a foot of saw-dust makes a good bottom. A very satisfactory substitute is made by laying small round poles in the bottom of the ice-house covered with straw and the straw covered with saw-dust about a foot deep. It is impossible for the air to come up through a foot of wet saw-dust in sufficient quantities to do much harm.

There is a good deal in packing the ice in the house to make it keep well. It should be put in during cold weather and all the chinks carefully filled with broken ice and the whole mass well frozen together by pouring on water. By doing this very carefully the ice can be frozen together almost solid so the air will all be forced out.

There should be a space of a foot between the ice and the sides of the house all around and this foot filled in with saw-dust tamped down. The saw-dust should be at least a foot deep on top of the ice; eighteen inches is better.

A great deal of ice is lost during the spring months when the weather is getting warm, but not warm enough to require the use of ice in the refrigerator. During these weeks the ice-house is forgotten, and it melts a little and settles. The settling process opens cracks in the wet saw-dust and some of these cracks will extend through to the ice. After the house is filled and covered with saw-dust it should have attention at least once a week. If the sawdust is kept packed down well all around and on top the ice cannot melt very much.

There are other details to think about, such as ventilation and shade. It is a great help to have the house shaded by a large tree or another building. When the sun beats down hot on top of the roof the temperature inside the building is a great deal higher than it would be with the roof shaded. If shade cannot be had a small opening in each gable will induce a current of air and help materially.

In choosing the location convenience in using the ice should be considered in preference to convenience in filling the ice-house, because the filling is done in a day or two whereas the unloading process occupies several months and requires innumerable trips between the kitchen and the ice-house.

Cheap Ice House—A137.

About the cheapest way of building an ice house that looks all right is shown in plan A 137. It is twelve feet square on the ground and twelve feet high to the eaves and the roof is steep enough to give head room for packing the ice clear up to the plates or above them.

The house will hold a cube of ice ten feet in diameter and leave room for a foot of saw dust all around. There are three hinged doors in front and inside of the doors are loose boards to hold the saw-dust in place. These boards may be taken out one at a time as the ice is used.

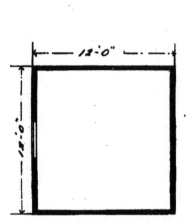

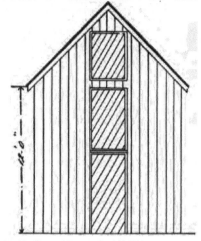

PLAN AND ELEVATION OF ICE HOUSE

Two Small Ice-Houses.

A small practical ice house that is not expensive to build is shown in plan A 104.

It is twelve by sixteen feet long on the ground and twelve feet to the plates. This house will hold more ice than a farmer needs for his own use, unless he has a dairy. In keeping milk, and especially where butter is made, a good deal of ice

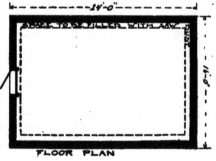

CROSS SECTION   FLOOR PLAN

can be used to advantage in hot weather.

In building a house like this it is a good plan to make the foundation of cinders six inches or a foot deep on ground that is well drained. Cover the cinders with a thin layer of straw and put sawdust about a foot deep over the straw. You cannot have a better foundation for ice than a bottom built in this way. There is a light frame work of two by fours built on sills six by six with outside boarding of drop siding nailed over tarred paper and covered

you have to use the material that you can get. If you can't get anything better than straw it will answer the purpose, but it requires more attention than better material.

These three plans cover the ice house question so far as the farmer is concerned. There are many other kinds of houses built on dif-

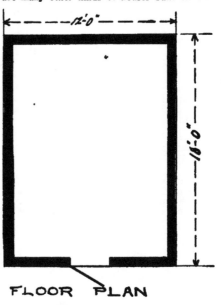

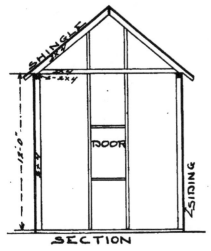

with a good shingled roof. The inside is ceiled up with any kind of rough boarding with joints tight enough to hold sawdust.

Plan A 103 is built the same way, the only difference being in the size on the ground. If a farmer has a very large dairy a house sixteen by twenty-four feet perhaps would not be too large. It often happens that farmers have an opportunity to sell several tons of ice at a good price if they have more than they want for their own use.

In some parts of the country it is difficult to get sawdust. Probably the next best material to preserve ice is marsh grass or marsh hay. The reason why marsh hay is better than tame hay or straw is because the shell of the stalk is tougher and thinner, and when it gets damp it mats down closely and keeps the air from the ice. Of course,

ferent plans, some of which are on an elaborate scale with expensive machinery for filling and other machinery to take the ice out, but it is not our province to take up questions of this nature. Ice is such a comfort on the farm, and in many localities it may be had so easily in winter, that every farmer should provide his family with such a luxury. People living in the city pay high prices for small quantities delivered each day, and they usually find it necessary to scrub the kitchen floor after each visit from the ice man, but they consider ice indispensable. For some reason farmers have been very slow to avail themselves of the opportunity to have ice on tap at all times. There is another plan that may interest some farmers who would like to have a little better house, and it will be found on the next page.

Refrigerator Ice House—A118.

An ice house with a cold storage room is shown in plan (A118). The walls are

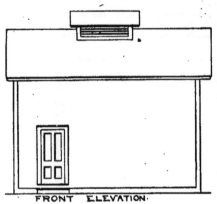

FRONT ELEVATION

built hollow with paper inside and out.
In the cold storage department there are several thicknesses of paper in the inner wall to make the dead air space as tight

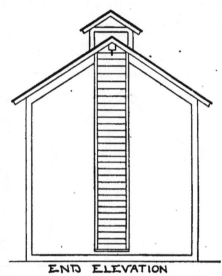

END ELEVATION

as possible. If you have ever undertaken to make an absolutely dead air space you understand the difficulty, or the impossibility of doing it. There is sure to be a crack somewhere to let the air through,

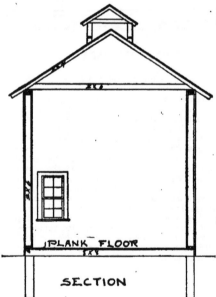

PLANK FLOOR

SECTION

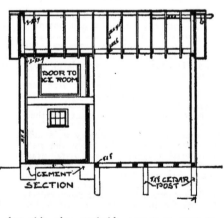

DOOR TO ICE ROOM

CEMENT
SECTION

CEDAR POST

but this plan probably comes as near to it as is necessary.
When an ice house is made as tight as

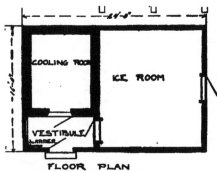

FLOOR PLAN

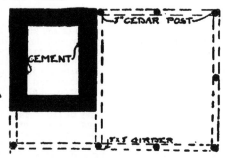

FOUNDATION PLAN

this it is necessary to let the top air out. For this reason a ventilator is built in the

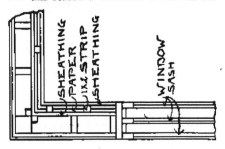

roof to encourage a circulation of air between the upper ceiling and the shingles. In this arrangement the cold storage department is supplied with ice as needed by putting in a quantity, say once a week.

The construction of an ice house like this requires good workmanship. You will need the best mechanic in the neighborhood and it will pay to read up on cold storage before you start in. If it is made just right it will be a great comfort and satisfaction, but if it is not made right it will cause a great deal of trouble and be a continuous annoyance.

Elevated Granary—A107.

Farmers have more use for granaries than formerly. There are two reasons for this, one is that more stock is kept on the

and it pays to hold grain to sell later. Then, more attention is now being paid to seed. A grain house like this with a place for scales and a fanning mill is a very valuable addition to any farm. The different kinds of grain may be stored in the bins at

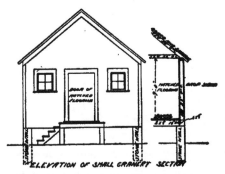

ELEVATION OF SMALL GRANARY SECTION

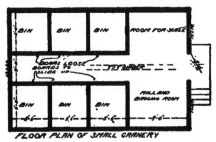

FLOOR PLAN OF SMALL GRANARY

farm and it is necessary to have grain the year round, another is that owing to a shortage of cars and speculation in grain, prices are not always satisfactory in the fall

threshing time and run through the fanning mill when taken to the warehouse for sale. By rigging the mill carefully a small proportion of the largest, heaviest grains may be retained for seed without adding anything to the cost. A good mill that will select say one bushel out of ten of the kind of grain that you want to sow and do it while blowing the chaff out of the grain you are selling without interfering with the grade is a valuable mill, but there are just such fanning mills made and their cost is little if any more than the common kind of the market.

In this scale room wires may be stretched for hanging the empty bags when not wanted. By sinking the scales in the floor each bag may be weighed as it is loaded. This is best done by having a two-wheeled bag truck and a counter weight on the scale beam so that the net weight may be written down each time without taking the time to calculate.

Great care should be taken in building a granary to have it rat proof. The wall of course must go below frost and it is a good plan to put a three-inch tile all around the bottom on the outside which answers for drainage as well as to keep rats from burrowing under the wall. Some farmers

object to a platform in front of the door just on account of rats, but if the door is made heavy and made to fit tight with a bit of hoop iron at the bottom, rats will not get in that way if the door is kept shut. It is difficult to arrange a plan of getting in and out conveniently without a platform. The door is too high to step up and if you have a stair to reach it you might just as well have a good loading platform as a cheap shaky affair. A grain house should bet set up well from the ground for two reasons, it should be the height of the wagon for easy loading and unloading and it should be high and dry because grain should be kept from all unnecessary moisture. There is moisture enough in the air in damp weather anyhow without taking chances on moisture from the ground.

The doors to the bins are made of loose boards dropped into grooves so that one board may be put in or taken out as required. A little extra expense put into the quality of the flooring is money well laid out. The floor should be free from shake and fairly free from knots, at least there should be no black knots.

Rat Proof Granary—A141.

Next to a chicken house, a granary offers the greatest inducement for rats. A dry floor and one that is rat proof may be made by excavating for the foundation

the exact depth, make the pit a little deeper than necessary, because the scales may be easily blocked up. At the edges around the sills and outside of the cinders let the con-

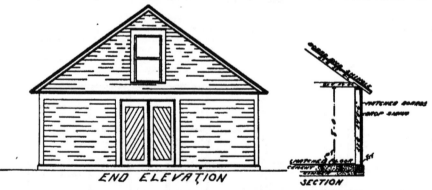

END ELEVATION   SECTION

about six inches deep. Then pound in about three or four inches of cinders and lay the sills and joists on the cinders and fill in the spaces between the joists with concrete. In framing the joists build a pit for the scales just deep enough to let them in flush with the floor. If you don't know

crete project down and outward about a foot all around.

Concrete for this purpose may be made with very little cement, say, one part cement, three parts sand and four parts gravel or broken stone pounded down so that no stones project above the joists and strike it off level with a straight-edge. Do this work about a week before the sides of the building are put up and sprinkle the concrete every day so it will dry properly. The studding is then set up in the usual way and matched boarding put on the outside of the studding, and the boarding covered with siding in the usual way. This construction leaves the studding exposed on the inside of the bins, so that a dog or cat can easily reach rats or mice that find their way inside. Hollow walls make harbors for vermin, but this construction leaves them no protection. There is a window in the back end of the alley, and another one over the door in front. The doors are made heavy and swing out. They close against heavy jambs so that rats and mice have very little encouragement to eat their way in around the door.

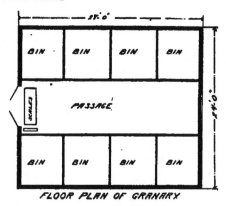

FLOOR PLAN OF GRANARY

Single Corn Crib—A106.

Sometimes a single corn crib is preferable to a double one. The corn keeps better in a single crib because the air circulates all around. Sometimes corn will mould in the center, even in a good crib that is properly constructed and not too wide. Sometimes farmers bore the floor

be any length, but the posts should be not more than eight feet apart.

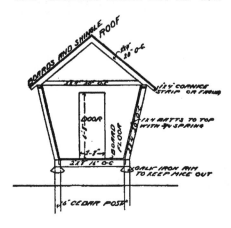

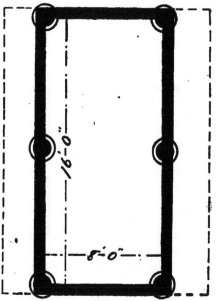

full of holes to help the ventilation, but this lets the shelled corn through and as dirt settles to the bottom the holes get easily covered over, and it is doubtful if they help very much. A better plan is to have the sides carefully constructed and to have the corn in a good condition when it is put in crib. A crib built after this plan may

SMALL CORN CRIB

Double Corn Crib—A120.

A double corn crib with storage room overhead and a driveway in the center is shown in this illustration. A peculiar feature of this plan is the siding which is split from two by fours with a band saw in such a way as to get three pieces of siding from of the studding which is placed twenty-four inches apart. It is impossible to get corn enough into a crib of this height to break the slats or shove them out. Corn cribs should not be more than six feet wide, because corn will mold in a crib that is too

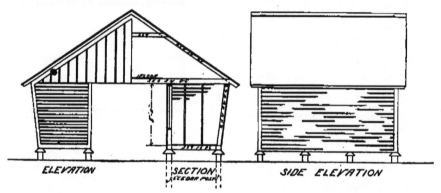

ELEVATION   SECTION   SIDE ELEVATION

one strip. After the siding is ripped out it is run through a sticker to give the curve as shown in the detail drawing. This is an extra protection against beating storms and it is supposed to encourage a draft of fresh wide; the air cannot get through to dry it.

The driveway in the center of a crib like this is very useful. There is room for a wagon or two and there may be pegs to hang a great many farm implements such

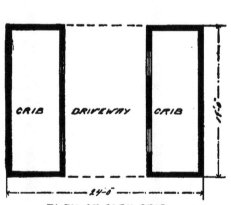

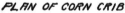

PLAN OF CORN CRIB

DETAIL OF SIDING

air up through each opening for the benefit of the corn. The strips are nearly an inch thick on the lower edge, making them strong enough to hold the corn by being well nailed with wire nails on the outside as neck-yokes, extra whiffle-trees, chains and hand tools of all kinds. The loft overhead makes good storage for lumber, and there is no better place for seed corn than to hang it by wires from the collar beams.

The tin pans turned up-side-down over the tops of the cedar posts will bother the rats most of the time, although they sometimes find a way to get in. Probably carelessness in leaning something against the crib helps them up in the majority of cases. Rats and mice are often carried into the crib with the corn. They are sharp enough to get into a bushel crate and stay there until they are carried inside. In this way a farmer often populates his own corn crib with rats or mice without intending to.

Another Double Corn Crib—A105.

An old fashioned style double corn crib with a drive between and a roof to cover both cribs is shown in plan (A105). This crib is set on cedar posts planted three and one-half feet in the ground and set up two and one-half feet above ground to be out of the way of mice and rats. The space between the two cribs makes a convenient place to store a couple of wagons. The side opening from the center passage, but if the space is desirable for wagon storage

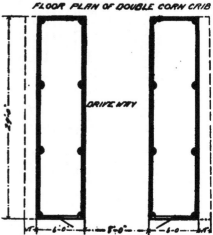

FLOOR PLAN OF DOUBLE CORN CRIB

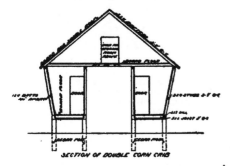

SECTION OF DOUBLE CORN CRIB

doors being at the end, the center space is left free for this purpose. A good many cribs built on this plan have the doors inside the doors are built at the end as shown. The storage room overhead will be found useful on any farm.

Round Corn Crib—A142.

So far as the size is concerned there is more room in a round corn crib than in any other shape made with the same amount of material. The building is easily constructed because it is all plain work and it is rat proof because it is set up two feet from the ground on cement posts.

The posts are made by digging holes in the ground three and one-half feet deep and about eight inches in diameter. Lengths of eight-inch pipe made of galvanized iron are used to carry the cement two feet above the ground. Before commencing it is necessary to strike a common level at the surface of the ground, so that when the pipes are all set up the tops of them will be the same height. The post above the ground and the post under ground should all be made at the same time so that the cement will unite into one solid post.

The floor plan shows the way the joists are laid and the circles represent the girts to which the 1x4 upright pieces are nailed. As the crib is sixteen feet in diameter it is necessay to have a ventilator in the middle. Ordinarily it is not advisable to have a body of corn more than six or seven feet in diameter. By making the inner circle three feet we have six and one-half feet between the inner strips and the outer strips, and as there is no floor over the joists in the center the air can pass up through the three-foot ventilator easily.

The round girts may be made in two

ways, either by using thin stuff and nailing one layer upon the other, breaking joints, or they may be ripped out of two-inch planks. If ripped out of planks a single

The roof is supported by a similar girt and this upper girt or plate is supported by extending some of the one by four pieces above the others as shown in the drawing. These extension strips may be doubled or two by fours may be used at these places. The crib is twelve feet high to the plate. An air space is left all around and this air space is big enough to shovel corn through.

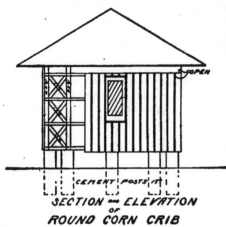

SECTION — ELEVATION
OF
ROUND CORN CRIB

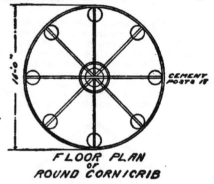

FLOOR PLAN
OF
ROUND CORN CRIB

saw-cut through each piece of plank will shape the sections, cut as shown in the diagram. Use two-inch plank ten inches wide cut to four-foot lengths. Make segments

Of course the corn is put in at the door and at the opposite window until the crib is pretty well filed.

The roof itself is a very simple affair. It

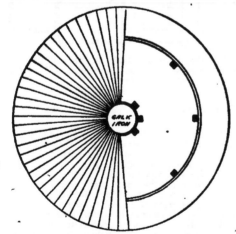

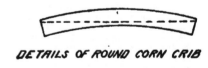

DETAILS OF ROUND CORN CRIB

enough to build up all the girts necessary by ripping the short planks lengthwise through the middle, then rip again on the curved line. The finished girts are about 4x4¾ inches. There is very little waste.

is supported by the plate and the ventilator shaft. The roof boards are twelve feet long and cut eleven inches at the wide end and one inch at the upper end or narrow end. These boards are nailed in place and the cracks battened. The center is easily filled in with sheet of galvanized iron having a cut reaching from one edge to the center. Such a roof if kept painted will last a long time. It is very light, cheap and easily made.

For Grain and Corn.

A cheap building to hold grain and corn is shown in design No. A128. It is a low building with studding only ten feet long, but that is about as high as a person cares to pitch corn or threshed grain. Just ordinary one by four pine strips spaced to ¾ inch are nailed on the outside of two by four studding to make the corn crib but the wheat and oat bins of course are made tight all around and a little extra work is put on the floor.

There is considerable side pressure in a

FRONT ELEVATION.

a building thirty by forty feet. Thirty feet is wide enough for convenience either in

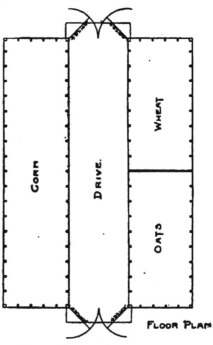

CORN   DRIVE.   WHEAT   OATS

FLOOR PLAN

wheat bin which must be guarded against by using a few extra braces, but heavy timbers are unnecessary in a bin the size of this one. This building may be floored overhead for storage or the bins may be left open to the roof. By leaving the space open the building will be lighted sufficient by the small window in each gable.

It is not intended to floor the driveway unless it is needed when using a fanning mill to clean grain, but the building would be all the better for having a good solid floor the full size. This plan provides for

building or for use afterwards, but of course it may be any length.

Wagon Shed—A108.

A wagon shed twenty feet wide and forty feet long, like the one in the plan illustrated, is a useful building to have on any farm. One thing is important about a wagon shed and that is to have the entrance wide enough to get things in and out easily and quickly. This double door gives an opening ten feet wide which is very good for small implements, but some binders require about sixteen. The door entering an implement shed must be high enough to let in the highest implements used on the farm, and there must be no cross timbers inside lower than the top of the door.

The farmer building the shed will know whether he wants to house a binder under full sail or whether he wants to take it apart, and will of course build a doorway accordingly.

Implement sheds, like all other buildings, should be designed for what is to be required of them. An implement shed is a necessity on every farm, but some farmers want to house threshing machines and traction engines, while others want a shed to hold mowers, plows, cultivators, a wagon or two and perhaps a few barrels and other truck. A large building, of course, would answer for everything but it is not necessary to build bigger than a man wants.

A good many tool houses are built without floors, but the extra cost of the floor

and machinery require repairing which is easily done in a building like this when you have a good floor to work on. Odd days in winter may be profitably spent in such a building with a few carpenter's tools, a

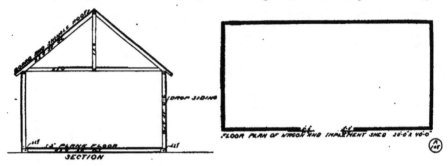

SECTION

is more than offset by the dryness and freedom from rust of the machinery. Wagons

paint brush and an assortment of paints and oils.

Implement Shed—A148.

An implement shed sixteen feet wide by forty-eight feet long is given in plan (A148). This shed really is built in sixteen-foot sections and may be carried to any length, but this size will hold the implements and machinery on an ordinary farm and leave room at one end for a work bench and repair shop.

The front is all doors so that any part of the shed may be opened and any imple-

ment removed without the work of getting it past some of the others. We have all had experience in crowded quarters for farm machinery. We have been obliged to call all the male men together and occa-

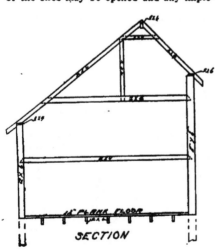

SECTION

ELEVATION

sionally invite the women to help get a grain drill out from behind harrows, plows, cultivators and other machinery. One reason why farm machinery is neglected is because farmers have no place to keep it. It is not repaired when it should be for the same reason. It is quite a job to do a simple piece of repair work if you haven't the tools or the room in which to do it, but anybody can clean up machinery and oil or paint it if they have a comfortable place to work in and the tools to work with.

same head room is then needed. A truss is formed at each bent with the rafters to prevent the building from spreading. The two by four nailers shown in the detail drawing is intended for the end bents only.

In the end of the shed most convenient

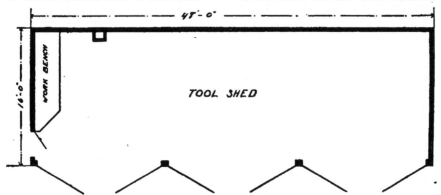

The front part of this shed is built higher than the back part in order to leave head room. If you want to get in with a binder with the reel on, or to house a threshing machine or traction engine, you need about ten feet to the top of the doors, but you don't need so much height to the back end. The doors in this plan are ten feet high and the cross girts are the same height because it is sometimes necessary to move the machines lengthwise of the shed and the

a good solid bench should be rigged up and fitted with a good vise. At the back of this bench there should be a long low window similar to those used in blacksmith shops all over the country. The bench should be heavy, solid and at least three feet wide. There should be a good floor, especially in the bench end of the building, and it is a good plan to put up a chimney and have a stove there.

Tank House—A144.

Every farm should have a windmill and every windmill should have a tank house connected with pipes in such a way as to

keep a continuous supply of water for the stock. Tank houses are wet things and it is better not to have one inside of a barn.

PLAN OF TANK HOUSE

A tank house is necessary to shade the tank so the sun won't spoil it, to shade the water in summer to keep it cool and to protect it from frost in winter.

Plan (A144) shows a snug little house, tightly built with. paper in the walls and a tank inside six feet high, four feet wide and twelve feet long. In the winter time a space between the sides of the tank and the sides of the building may be filled in with manure to keep water from freezing.

Pipes from the bottom of the tank to the watering troughs are connected with valves either underground or in boxes that are covered with manure. The valves have long stems so they may be turned from outside the building, or by opening the little door and reaching in.

Tower Tank House—A145.

Where a water pressure is wanted it often is a good plan to put the water tank in the windmill tower. In plan (A145) the tank is shown in the dotted lines. It is placed ten feet above the ground and the tank itself is fourteen feet high by ten feet in diameter at the bottom.

In placing a tank like this it is necessary to carry a three inch pipe through the tank and pass the pump shaft through this pipe. The pipe is screwed into a flange at the bottom and the flange is bolted to the bottom of the tank to make it thoroughly water tight. The pipe must be steadied at the top and the shaft must have a bearing, both above the tank and below it so it won't scrape on the pipe. The well and pump of course are directly under the tank in the center of the tower.

The outside boarding is made double and lined with paper to be warm in winter.

There is generally some drip from a tank placed like this, for which reason the room below is seldom made use of for any purpose, but a few farmers have utilized this room for a bath room. They make a cement bottom with a drain to carry off the surplus water and put in a shower bath, connected with a pipe from the tank. A shower bath is the most convenient and probably the most healthful of any kind of a bath. At any rate it is easily kept clean.

There is no reason why a farmer or his men should be denied the privilege of getting a bath when they want it. There are bath rooms in almost all city houses and there should be bathing conveniences on every farm. By placing a stove in this room under the tank it could be made comfortable in winter as well as summer, and a stove with a water heater attached to the tank would give a water pressure so that the shower could be made any temperature desired.

TANK HOUSE

Scale House—A187.

This is a photograph of a good scale house covering an eight by fourteen foot platform, four ton scale. The building is fourteen by sixteen feet base with doors

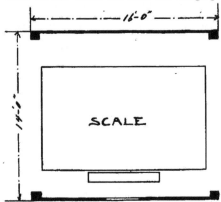

twelve feet high, allowing a large load of hay to be driven in upon the scales. The sides of the house are used for hanging

and placing tools and other small articles not wanted in the barn.

Every up-to-date farm should have a good pair of scales big enough to weigh a load of hay or a drove of hogs or sheep. Enough money is lost on every farm by guessing at weights to pay for a good set of scales, and besides this there is a great satisfaction in knowing what things weigh.

In feeding cattle, hogs or sheep for market weighing at regular periods is extremely valuable. It is impossible to know whether stock is doing as well as it should do unless tab is kept on the increase in weight.

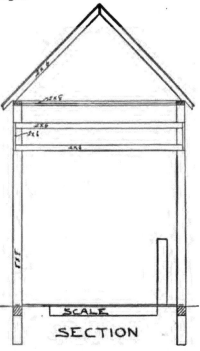

SECTION

After this scale house is built make a good solid rack to surround the scales to pen up stock at weighing time. Make the rack high enough to hold horses, strong enough to hold a bull and tight enough for hogs.

16'-0"

14'-0"

SCALE

PLAN

Cheap Smoke House—A149.

It is not necessary to do without a smoke house on a farm. A small building that will answer the purpose may be had with very little outlay. The plan (A149) shows a little wooden smoke house eight by ten feet with sides eight feet high. It

roof. It is better, however, to make a good shingle roof, then you have something that will last as long as you want it. For boarding you just take sixteen foot boards and cut them in two in the middle. For the front and back use twelve foot lumber and

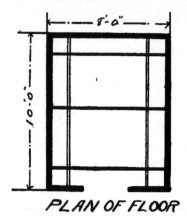

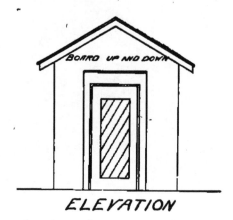

PLAN OF FLOOR   ELEVATION

is big enough to hold as many hams and shoulders as farmers' families usually require with once filling, but it is an easy matter to fill the house the second time if you have the meat.

This little house requires no frame work at all. All you need is a four by four for sills and a two by four for plates and some more two by fours for rafters. You can even dispense with the rafters, except the two end pairs, if you want to make a board

the waste pieces work in for roof boards if shingles are used.

A smoke house like this is not tight enough to keep the meat in after being smoked. It is better to wrap it in paper, then roll it up in thin cotton and sew it up. You mustn't leave a place for a fly to crawl in. You must then hang the packages with strings, perfectly free. They must not touch each other and they must not touch anything else. They need a cool place, but not damp.

Cement Block Smoke House—A147.

Every farm should have a smoke house, the better the house the more satisfactory will be the meat. The plans shown of (A147) is for a house constructed of cement blocks. It should be placed conveniently near the house on a raise of ground and a foundation started below the frost line. A trench should be dug, say 3½ feet deep partly filled with concrete made of one part of Portland cement, two and one-half parts sand and five parts of broken stone or gravel, ramming or puddling carefully. If plenty of sand may be conviently had, it would be a good plan to secure a block machine and have the blocks

made on the ground. In making the concrete blocks, use a mixture of one part Portland cement, two and one-half parts sand and five parts of crushed stone or gravel. The use of crushed stone or coarse material for the back of the block saves a great deal of cement and at the same time gives a much better block than where sand and cement alone are used. Blocks made of sand and cement alone and merely dampened are not concrete blocks, but on the contrary are simply sand blocks. The very term of concrete suggests coarse material and plenty of water. Great care should be taken in mixing the different aggregates and they should be mixed thoroughly dry and after they have been thoroughly mixed add water. After the blocks have been made they should be set aside to be cured, and while curing, they should be sprayed thoroughly

ELEVATION

from seven to ten days. This spraying should commence about twelve hours after the block has been made. Blocks should never be used in building until they are from twenty to thirty days old.

Farm cured meats are a great luxury if the hogs are properly grown on pasture. With a house like this and good pork to start with, a farmer can supply his table with good home-made bacon, hams and shoulders the year round.

The best smoke is made from green maple wood. Probably clean corn cobs come next. With a smoke house thoroughly well built to keep out flies and other in-

sects the meat may be smoked in the spring and left in the smoke house all summer. By way of precaution a very little smoke may be started once or twice a month or some of the meat may be covered with paper and cloth. Very much depends on the house. If the house is too dry there will be too much evaporation and the meat will become dry; if the house is too damp it will be inclined to mould. If it is intended to keep the meat in the house after the smoking process is completed it will be necessary to fit the door

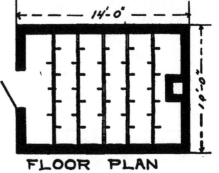

FLOOR PLAN

very carefully. The frame must have a couple of ridges all around and cement worked in tight between these ridges to make tight joints. The ventilator on top must be fitted with a fine screen. Two screens would be better. A coarse galvanized screen on top and a fine screen inside at the bottom.

The plates and rafters must be laid in fresh cement mortar on top of the wall. All spaces between rafters are filled in so as to prevent cracks or openings of any kind. Cross poles to support the meat are made of four by fours with half inch pegs inserted from the sides. The pegs are set at an angle of about thirty degrees. This will permit hanging the pieces of meat in the old fashioned way of cutting a slit in the skin in the bone end. If strings are preferred the same kind of peg may be used. Nails are not to be recommended for this purpose.

Good Hog House—A109.

In building a hog house it is necessary to consider convenience in getting the hogs in and out, to provide means for loading them into wagons and a place for heating

water and to do the work of killing. This plan offers an opportunity to back the wagon up to the rear door for loading and a room in the front end away from the pens is arranged for a feed room and slaughter house.

Provision is made for moving hogs from one pen to another by having cleats in the alley for holding sliding doors.

Hogs thrive better when animals of the same size are penned together. Some grow faster than others and it is sometimes desirable to select out one or two from certain pens. That is the time when the alley door will be appreciated. Another good thing about this hog house is the swinging front of the pens which swings back over the trough and prevents interference when

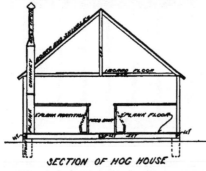

SECTION OF HOG HOUSE

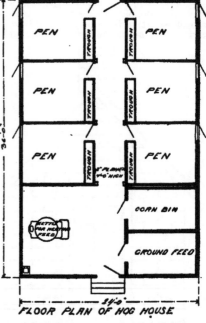

FLOOR PLAN OF HOG HOUSE

putting in the feed. The partitions next to the feed room run to the ceiling but the partitions between the pens are only four feet high.

There is no cornice to the roof. The openings above the plates between the raft-ers are left for ventilation. This hog house will accommodate about forty hogs by housing from six to eight in a pen, which is thick enough; if more are penned together they pile up and smother each other.

Hog House and Corn Crib—A140.

Hogs and corn may both be kept in the same house economically by building a house like the one shown in plan A 140. To facilitate getting the corn in it is an advantage to put the house on a hillside

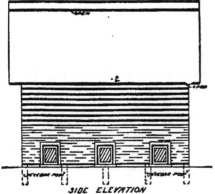

SIDE ELEVATION

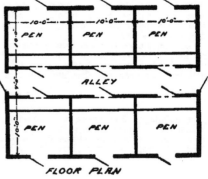

FLOOR PLAN

with the wagon road on the upper side and use a schute to run corn into the house.

The building is set up from the ground about a foot on posts, and pens are made on both sides of an alley in the usual way.

sary to let the air through. A couple of slatted partitions or even a pile of empty bushel crates will answer the purpose.

This corn house is ventilated in a peculiar way, as is shown in the cut; refer to

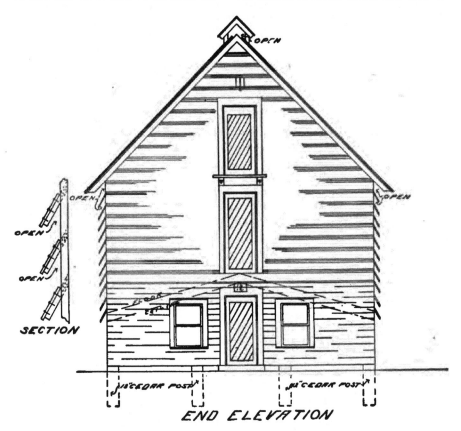

END ELEVATION

Above the hog house is a solid floor to hold the corn, built slanting each way from the center, leaving about seven feet head room in the middle over the feeding alley and about five feet at the sides of the building. There are two reasons for building the floor in this way, one is to get the corn down as low as possible and the other is to divide it into two parts to prevent moulding. If the house is filled with corn to the roof some other division would be necessary.

both the general plan and the section detail. To prevent the corn from getting out through the wide spaces, poultry netting is tacked on the inside of the studding.

The peculiarity of the floor construction needs careful attention when building, otherwise the sloping floor might settle in the middle sufficiently to push the sides out. By running the alley partitions up to the upper floor joists the upper floor may be supported so thoroughly as to prevent any such trouble.

Cheap Hog House.

The cheapest kind of a hog house is shown in plan (A 122). It is only seven feet six inches wide, but it may be any length. This house is thirty-one feet six inches long because this length is covered by two sixteen-foot joists.

boards cut in two in the middle. Each sixteen-foot section will make two pens nearly eight feet square which will hold from five to seven or eight pigs according to size. It rests on posts set three feet into the ground and one foot above to keep the floor

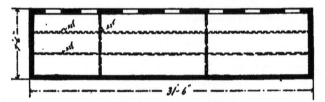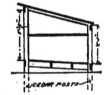

PLAN AND SECTION OF HOG HOUSE

Even on well regulated hog farms where there is a good solid hog house this shed affair will be found useful to hold the overflow. It often happens that shotes in fall are kept in a muddy feed lot or sold too soon for lack of just such shelter as this to hold them while being finished. Beginners in the hog business could not do better than to build a little cheap hog house like this to start with.

The seven and one-half-foot width permits of roofing the shed with sixteen-foot

dry. Four two by six joists run lengthwise of the building and the floor boards run crosswise and slant back for easy cleaning. A space is left between the floor boards and the boarding at the back so a scraper may be used. In cold weather this space is closed by a hinged board which drops down on the inside. This precaution is necessary because a cold draft on the floor is a very bad thing for hogs. This little hog house doesn't run into very much money but it is a very useful practical affair.

Stave Silo—A157.

The cheapest way to make a satisfactory silo is to build it of two-inch staves with a cement foundation and pit. Stave silos don't last forever, probably their average usefulness is somewhere between five and ten years. It will vary according to the material used in the construction, the care with which they are built and the protection they receive afterward, especially when not filled. The best stave silos will go to pieces if the hoops are not kept tight when the silo is empty.

The most convenient height to make a stave silo is thirty-two feet above the wall. This gives an opportunity to use sixteen-foot stuff to advantage. In building a silo sixteen feet in diameter it is only necessary to use two lengths of staves, a short length eight feet and a long length sixteen feet in order to break joints at different heights. If larger silos are built it is a good plan to use enough four-foot and twelve-foot length of staves so that you have only one joint

to two solid staves on one level. Where only two lengths are used, as in this plan, the joints and solid staves come alternately, but even this makes a very strong structure when the hoops are pulled up tight, as they should be at all times.

The staves should not be wider than eight inches. The edges should be straight and true, the bevel carefully made on a sticker and trued up with a hand jointer by a competent workman. The bevel is very important. Where the edges of the staves come together the joint should be perfect from inside to outside and from top to bottom of the silo.

It very often happens that it is not convenient to use staves all of the same width. They may be from six to eight inches wide, but they must come in pairs or sets of three of the same width together. Where staves are used of different widths the system of numbering shown in the drawing will be found very useful. Staves are all cut to size and length and numbered; they can then be loaded on a wagon and hauled to the building site and laid·out on the ground in proper order. There will be about seventy-five eight-inch staves in a silo sixteen feet in diameter. The door frame takes up about three feet of the circle.

In making the door frame ladder, use the

in place by lag screws turned into the timber. The outside boarding of the doors is double to make a firm hold for the lag screws. It is a slower job to put the doors on when they are fastened in this way, but

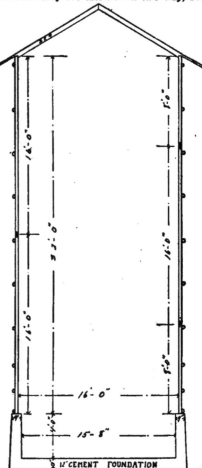

ELEVATION OF SILO   CROSS SECTION OF SILO

best material you can get and have it framed square and solid with good jambs well fitted for the inside door panel to shut against. It is almost impossible to make a silo door tight enough.

The doors in this plan are built like refrigerator doors. They are put on and held

it is only necessary to change them twice a year.

A hoop passes around the silo between each door. These hoops are made in sections, each length about sixteen feet six inches long, as this allows for the lap and the take up of the threads at the yokes.

There is a cast iron yoke at each meeting of the hoops, as shown in the detail drawing.

The bottom of the silo is made of ce-

clear. The walls are nine inches thick on top.

In starting the woodwork first set up the ladder door frame on the center of the ce-

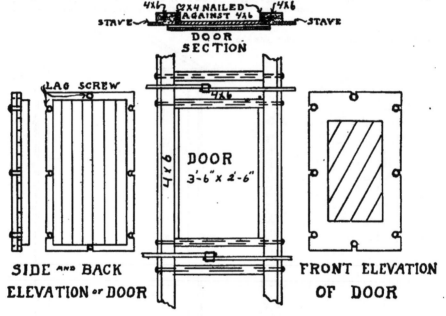

ELEVATION OF DOOR FRAME

ment. A round hole is dug seventeen feet eight inches in diameter. A cement wall is built around the outside of this hole a foot thick at the bottom and nine inches at

ment wall. Make it plumb and stay-lath it in place and put on plenty of braces so it can't move. Then set up the staves, starting at one side of the ladder with number

1	1				
2B	2B			2T	2T
		3	3		
4B	4B			4T	4T
		5	5		
6B	6B			6T	6T
		7	7		
8B	8B			8T	8T
		9	9		

STAVES NUMBERED and LETTERED

the top and five feet high. A twelve-inch bottom is put in at the same time so that the pit when finished is four feet deep and fifteen feet eight inches in diameter in the

one. Set the staves on end on the center of the wall or a little outside of the center. This is important because when you commence to tighten the hoops the staves must draw in and you want about two inches of wall on the inside after the staves are drawn tight. You shouldn't have more than two inches because you don't want a shelf at the top of the wall to prevent the silage from settling.

It will be noticed that the hoops are placed much closer together at the bottom than they are further up. It seems more

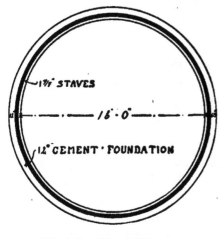

PLAN OF SILO

difficult to keep a silo tight at the bottom; there is more pressure on it. When the sides are up and the hoops made tight the bottom should be finished all around, both inside and out, with rings of cement where the wooden staves meet the cement wall. Make this joint water tight if you possibly

can. Very often the juice from the corn will fill the pit and run over. Keep the liquid in if you possibly can.

The roof of the silo should be light and

BAND

IRON TONGUE

removable. You can't fill a silo full unless you have boards to set up to reach a few feet above the top. It will settle sometimes as much as ten feet. It is an advantage to

**74 1⅞" X 5" STAVES
IN A SILO 16-0 INSIDE DIAMETER**

take the top all off and to have boards six or eight feet long to set up around the top temporarily and fill to the top of these extra boards. It will settle enough then.

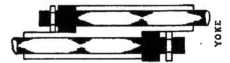

Where the ends of the staves meet make a saw-cut an inch deep. Have pieces of two-inch band iron cut just long enough to reach the width of the staves and use them for iron tongues to match the ends of the staves together.

DEPARTMENT
OF
LITTLE
FARM HELPS

FOLDING ROOSTS AND DROPPINGS BOARD.

A convenient hen roost and droppings board that will fold up against the wall out of the way is m a d e by nailing roosts across two supporting pieces as shown in the cut. The side supports are two and one-half feet long and are hinged to the wall. This gives room for three roosts. The droppings board is made to extend beyond the outside roosting pole about six or eight inches. Cleats are run along the outside bottom edges of the droppings board and bolts fasten the two legs to the supporting pieces of the roosts and to the cleats under the droppings board. The rig may be any length by putting in enough cross pieces to make it strong. The leg bolts must be the same distance from the wall in each case. The roosts are three and one-half feet above the floor. A pulley is attached to the wall and a rope run through it to lift the outfit and hold it up at cleaning time or during the day when it is not wanted for roosting. There should be a space of two or three inches between the droppings board and the wall and a trough placed under, so in cleaning the droppings will fall in the trough. To facilitate cleaning the board should be covered with sand or other material.

CHEAP FARM GATE.

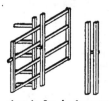

The cheapest practical farm gate that I have ever used is made without hinges. It is supported by a cleat and is opened by sliding it back three or four feet, then swinging it around. When shut it fits in between two posts and rests on another cleat to keep it up from the ground. It is necessary to brace the gate diagonally and it should have an upright place near the middle. Instead of mortising the bars into the end pieces it may be made by doubling inch pieces at each end and the middle and putting bolts through. Bolts are important because nails or screws will not hold in a gate. Use three-eighth inch bolts with washers. Have the bolts just long enough so that the nuts will screw down tight without projecting the bolts too much. Make the gate just a little higher than the fence and make the bottom board of the gate a little wider than the others. This gate is cheaply and easily made and is not liable to get out of order. It is quickly and easily opened or shut, requires no hinges, no latch, and I have never seen an animal ingenious enough to open it.

LAND LEVEL.

A cheap land level that would be found useful on any farm, is easily made out of three pieces of seven-eights in. pine three inches wide. The two outside legs or strips are twelve feet long, and the bottoms are placed sixteen and one-half feet apart, so that the level when finished will step a rod at a time. Nail the legs together at the top and nail the cross pieces on at one end. Then place the feet a rod apart on a level floor, put the level on the cross piece and raise or lower the loose end until it comes right. When it shows right, tack it and reverse the feet to prove. The same rig may be used by hanging a plumb-bob from the point at the top. Make a mark on the board where the line crosses when the feet are standing level.

CEMENT TROUGH.

Make a wooden mold the size and shape you want the trough. Make it in two pieces as shown in the cut. Put these pieces together and fasten with cleats tacked very lightly. Fill the form with a mixture of one part cement and one part sand. Let stand two hours, then with small trowel dig out the middle to trough shape. Smooth it carefully and set away for four days, then draw the nails, take off the cleats and turn upside-down, when the mold may be removed easily. Then make a thin paste of cement and apply with a whitewash brush. Go over the trough two or three times to make a nice finish.

CORN BINDER.

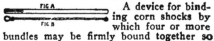

A device for binding corn shocks by which four or more bundles may be firmly bound together so the wind won't blow them down, may be made as follows: Cut a piece of broom handle twelve inches long, round both ends and smooth with sand-paper. Two inches from one end bore a quarter-inch hole about half way through the stick with a little groove extending from the hole to the end of the stick. This groove should be about half the depth of the stick. This is the binder. Now cut binding twine in lengths forty inches long. Double one end over to form a four-inch loop and finish the other end with a large knot. To use the binder drop the knot into the hole and stretch the cord along the groove cut for it. Pass the cord around the shock, run the free end through the loop in the cord and draw clear through giving the stick a backward twist to free it. The knotted end of the cord is held firmly by the loop and the spring of the stalks will keep the string taut. Where two bands are wanted two lengths of string will be necessary. The twine may be saved and used next year.

TO PULL OLD FENCE POSTS.

A piece of plank or two by four scantling about three feet long and a common logging chain will help a man and a pair of horses to lift a good many old fence posts out of the ground in a short time. The chain is hooked around the post to be lifted and the piece of plank set at an angle as shown in the cut.

CEMENT HITCHING POST.

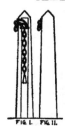

FIG. I.   FIG. II.

The size of the post is ten inches at the bottom and seven inches at the top, and it has an inch and a half gas pipe in the center with an elbow turned to one side, as shown in the cut. The post is made in a wooden mold, which is just a box of boards nailed together the size and shape of the post. This box is stood on end, the gas pipe put in place and the cement poured around it. There is a bolt through the elbow and on this bolt is a half-inch pipe coupling which answers for a pulley, over which the chain runs. There is a weight on the lower end of the chain just heavy enough to pull the chain back into the post when it is not in use. On the outer end

is a snap with a ring big enough to prevent the snap from going too far in. The cement is made of two parts sand and one part cement. The sand is very sharp and free from dirt.

STOCK SALT BOX.

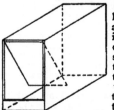

A salt box with a hinged front that animals may push in is a good rig. You can put a peck of salt in a box like this, set it up from the ground where it will keep dry and the animals will help themselves without further attention. They soon find how to push the door in and of course it swings shut of its own weight.

REMOVABLE HEN'S NEST.

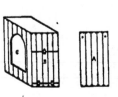

Cheap hens' nests that may be easily removed for cleaning are made from boxes picked up at the grocery store. I cut an opening in the side about twelve inches wide and fifteen inches high, shown at C, for the hen to enter. B is a door fastened with a button at the top. A shows the back of the box with two holes bored in the upper corners to hang on nails driven into the side of the hen house. The door B is handy for gathering the eggs and also for cleaning the nest boxes. I can lift off twenty-five such boxes, clean them and spray with some good louse-killer and put them back in thirty minutes. They cost me about six cents apiece and I can make one out of a box in about ten minutes.

CHEAP BATH.

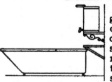

A room on the ground floor is required for this bath outfit so the water supply can be arranged by passing the hose through a small hole in the wall or window sash from the pump outside. Two large iron brackets are fastened to the wall at the end of the tub to hold the tank. Under this an oil stove is placed on a shelf at a suitable height so the heat from the oil stove will heat the water in the tank, when it is run from the faucet into the bath tub. An ordinary wash-boiler may be used in place of the tank, but a regular tank with a faucet attached is much more convenient and satisfactory. The waste pipe from the tub is connected with the drain from the kitchen sink.

BARB WIRE STRETCHER.

A hard wood stick about two feet long having a steel plate fastened to one end with a notch in it serves very well to stretch barb wire, if the lengths are not too long. The steel blade should be about an eighth of an inch thick and the notch filed in from the under side before the blade is fastened to the wooden bar. File the notch with a large three-cornered file, so the sides are beveled from the bottom, leaving a sharp cutting edge on the face side, then have the plate tempered. By working around a post considerable strain may be given to a single wire with this simple device.

AUTOMATIC POULTRY FEEDER.

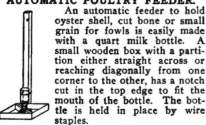

An automatic feeder to hold oyster shell, cut bone or small grain for fowls is easily made with a quart milk bottle. A small wooden box with a partition either straight across or reaching diagonally from one corner to the other, has a notch cut in the top edge to fit the mouth of the bottle. The bottle is held in place by wire staples.

HOME-MADE BAG TRUCK.

A great convenience for handling sacks of grain may be easily made at home. Two side bars four feet long, two inches wide and one and one-half inches thick are about right for the handles. Two discarded plow handles answer the purpose very well and two plow wheels or cultivator wheels may be used for rollers. The holes in the wheels will determine the kind of axle to use. If the holes are small an iron axle would be necessary, but if the holes are large a piece of hard wood will do for an axle. Gas pipe makes a good

axle and is easily drilled each side of the wheel so that washers and bolts may be used to keep the wheels in place, or the axle may be made the right length, the ends threaded and locknuts screwed on the ends. Two buggy thill irons will answer for the front. These may be bent to shape at the home forge (every farmer should have a home forge) but it is only a small job at the blacksmith shop. The irons should be bolted through the side pieces and a rod run across from one to the other in front to rest the sack on. The legs may be fastened to the under side with strap hinges so that they will fold back when the truck is hung up. Then paint it and put a hole in its ear so you may replevin it from the neighbor's flock if it runs away from home.

FLY KILLER.

This consists of a piece of screen wire about seven inches square. The handle is any light piece of wood split at one end to let in the screen and the screen is fastened with small wire nails. You can kill a fly every time with this rig because it does not create a breeze to blow the fly away. It does not smash the flies but just puts them permanently to sleep easily.

WAGON JACK.

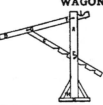

The upright A is made of two pieces three inches wide and an inch thick, just long enough to reach an inch above the bottom of the hind axle. B is a lever made of hard wood three feet long. C is about two feet long with notches every three inches E, F, G are iron bolts. D is twelve or fourteen inches long to prevent the jack from running forward when the wagon wheel is lifted. It is braced firmly to A.

PULLEY CLOTHES LINE.

A clothes line that may be used in stormy weather without going out doors is arranged with a post in the yard and three pulleys, one pulley on the post, one at the top of the window and one at the bottom of the window. Of course, only one line can be filled with clothes, as the other is required to move back and forth through the pulleys.

SURE GATE LATCH.

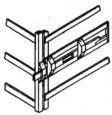

An ordinary sliding gate latch is made into a lock by cutting a notch into the back end and fitting a block on the gate bar to engage the notch. This arrangement is beyond the comprehension of the trickiest horse or cow.

DITCH CLEANER.

A road ditch cleaner, to be used in connection with a road drag, is made in the style of a snow-plough, but the hitch is different. Two planks, each two inches thick and ten inches wide, are used. The left-hand plank should be about six feet long and the right-hand plank seven or eight feet long. The left-hand plank is set vertical on edge and the right-hand plank is placed at an angle and shod with steel so that it works on the principle of a plough-share, digging the earth from the bottom of the ditch and shoving it up the side of the turnpike. The hitch is made adjustable by means of bolts as shown. Something by way of steering may be done by the driver by shifting his weight from one side to the other.

HAY RACK FOR SHEEP.

To keep hay clean when feeding sheep a rack with troughs at the side is a great advantage. Clover leaves and other fine stuff will be caught and eaten which otherwise would be wasted on the ground. It may be made any length, but

the longer the better. Sixteen foot two by fours are convenient for the frame. There should be about two center partitions to strengthen it.

MAIL BOX SUPPORT.

A mail box support that may be moved is easily made after this plan. The upright is a piece of four by four supported as shown by a frame work of lighter material. There is a board bottom to the frame to hold stones. By weighting the box the standard will remain in an upright position. This rig is convenient in winter when snow interferes with the regular roadway.

HOSE COUPLING FOR STEAM PIPE.

Sometimes it is necessary to couple two pieces of pipe together with a short hose. To prevent the hose blowing off, heat the ends of the pipe and work them out over the horn of an anvil in bell shape as shown in the cut. Then work the hose over and wire it tightly on each side of the joint.

ROLLER GATE.

A farm gate sixteen feet long, as it should be to get through easily with a hayrack, is too heavy to slide easily. There is a cast iron roller made for the purpose and sold in hardware stores. The cut shows how it is fastened to the posts so the gate slides halfway back. In a long gate there is always a center piece up and down with a diagonal brace running from the center to the front end of the gate. The posts are mortised to let in a two-inch block and the casting that holds the roller is let into this block and an iron washer slipped over the bolt so the casting will turn easily. As the washer is protected from the wet it may be kept oiled. My gate pulleys are mostly made from chain pulleys taken from old binders, but they must have a good deep flange.

CLOTHES RACK.

A clothes rack that is convenient for hanging little things on consists of two frames hinged together. I load it full of handkerchiefs and small things in the house and carry it out and hang it on the clothes line. It saves cold fingers in winter and when the clothes freeze fast it may be carried in to let them thaw. It is a time saver and it is convenient.

FEED BOX FOR YOUNG CHICKENS.

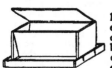

The box is two feet long and holds feed enough for forty chicks, feeding from both sides. The box can be raised or lowered according to the kind of feed, by putting round nails in the holes in the ends of the loose bottom. The sides of the feed box slope in and the bottom box or tray is three-quarters of an inch longer than the upper box that holds the feed. The same style of feed boxes may be used for full grown chickens by making them larger and longer.

MIRROR RAT TRAP.

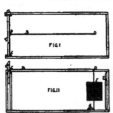

A rat trap with a looking glass in the back end to fool the rodents is made with a box about ten inches wide and ten or twelve inches high, and it may be two or three feet long. A light door (A) works easily in a groove between cleats (C C) in the front end. This door is held up by string (B) which passed through hole (D) in the top of the box and is attached to a piece of tin which is held down by the bait (G). The looking glass is at (E) against the back end of the box. When the rat looks in at the front door he sees his image in the mirror and thinks there is another rat coming to get the bait from the other way. He hurries to grab it first, releases string (B), the door drops and Mr. Rat is fast. There is a hole at (F) covered with wire netting so you can see the rat in the trap.

GATE FOR SMALL ANIMALS.

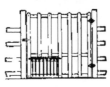

A small gate built into another gate for the accommodation of chickens or small pigs when you want to feed them in a separate trough is shown in this drawing. A sliding bar across the bottom will fasten the little gate shut.

BOTTLE DRINKING FOUNTAIN.

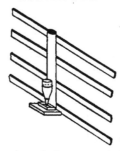

One quart and two quart glass bottles make the very best drinking fountains for poultry. They may be easily cleaned and you can see when they are clean. Use heavy wire for staples driven into a post or stake. The lower staple regulates the height of the fountain and the upper staple steadies it. Use a tin or earthenware dish under it. An old saucer works well. Block it up just high enough so the water won't overrun the dish.

SANITARY FEED TROUGH.

FEED TROUGH

To prevent fowls from tramping over feed, especially mashes, I have for a long time used these sanitary feed troughs. To make one, take an inch board about five feet long and from eight to ten inches wide; this is the upright center piece. Nail two boards the same length four or five inches wide against this upright, nailing at the bottom only, and one board on each side. Pull them open at the top three and one-half or four inches from the center board and nail on the end boards. The end boards should be at least a foot long to prevent the trough from turning over. With a half-inch bit bore holes in the top edge of center board three and one-half inches apart and drive in pegs six inches long. Troughs five feet long are handy to move, and, being double, makes ten feet of trough which is always clean, because the fowls can neither get into the trough nor rest on it. The hens line up like so many pigs and feed quietly.

WASH TANK.

It pays to wash vegetables before sending them to market. The smaller ones, such as radishes and celery, may be done in a small way with a box tank and a drip board. The tank should be connected with a water supply and have a waste pipe to empty it easily and quickly.

LIFTING GATE.

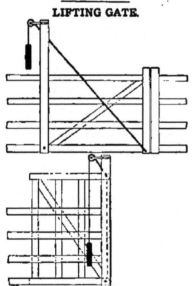

It sometimes happens that there is no room to swing a gate, or for some other reason it is not desirable to do so. This plan shows a solid gate that may be easily lifted because the pulley weight takes part of the lift and holds the gate open so there is no danger of it dropping unexpectedly to do damage. A barred gate is built in the usual way with a diagonal brace to keep it in shape. The high gate post is made double and the gate is fastened between by one bolt at the bottom, as shown in the cut. The iron that supports the pulley is bolted a little to one side of the opening so the cord may play easily and work free of the gate. The front or lower post also is made double, so when the gate shuts down it is held firmly in position between two posts at each end. A pin through the short posts and through the front part of the gate makes a very solid rig. Hogs cannot lift it and the most ingenious cattle cannot get it unfastened. Such a gate does not sag and it is easily opened. The posts, of course, should be firm and they should be plumb.

LOG DRAG.

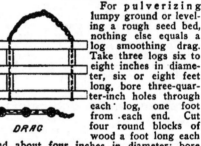

DRAG

For pulverizing lumpy ground or leveling a rough seed bed, nothing else equals a log smoothing drag. Take three logs six to eight inches in diameter, six or eight feet long, bore three-quarter-inch holes through each log, one foot from each end. Cut four round blocks of wood a foot long each and about four inches in diameter; bore these through lengthwise with a three-quarter auger and place them between the logs. Have made by a blacksmith two three-quarter-inch rods with an eye at one end and a nut and thread at the other end just long enough to pass through all the logs, and screw up tight behind. A hitching chain is hooked in the eyes of the bolts.

BOXES FOR SETTING HENS.

I have had good luck with boxes like this for setting hens. I cover the top with laths to protect the hens from interference. The box is large enough to hold the hen and chicks for a day or two after hatching. It contains three nests and is about three feet square on the ground and two feet high.

WHIP HANGER.

A hanger to keep carriage whips from curling is made with a strip of wood any length and about six inches wide with deep V-shaped notches cut a trifle wider at the bottom than they are at the top. The notches work better when made three inches deep and they should open an inch at the outer edge of the board and taper to nothing.

will tear the bag and if the hopper is too low you cannot fill the bag full.

AUTOMATIC POULTRY OILER.

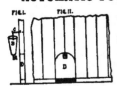

Kerosene is valuable to rid fowls of lice, but it is a disagreeable thing to use by hand. I have an automatic device that answers the purpose splendidly. I cut a gash in the bottom of a tin pail with a chisel. The cut is a close fit for an ordinary lamp wick. The wick is pulled through until it hangs down about three inches. It is hung in the small door that the chickens are obliged to pass through. Each chicken brushes against the hanging lamp wick and gets a drop of oil and the hen will do the rest.

TIN SCARECROW.

A device that works well to scare crows away from growing corn is made by looping a piece of tin loosely on an arm reaching out from a stake. The tin is very light and a slight breeze will keep it rattling. The ring is loose so the tin may be moved out or in and should be left just so the ends will strike against the stake. Bright tin moving and glistening in the sun is a very suspicious looking trap to a crow and its queer noise will frighten them away. It is not an experiment, it is an old tried device and it works all right.

GRAIN BAG HOLDER.

The upright is three and one-half feet long, one inch thick and fifteen inches wide. The bottom plank is two feet long. The hopper is the right size to fit the bag. Hooks are screwed into the sides of the hopper or nails are driven in and filed sharp. The hooks must be just high enough so the weight of the bag will rest on the bottom board. If the hopper is too high the weight

WOOD CARRIER.

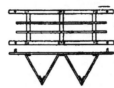

Carrying in wood is a chore that the boys do not like and the older folks begrudge the time. By making a rack with four legs, as shown in the illustration, enough wood may be carried in at one trip to last a day or two. The outside bars may be four or six feet long, the ends rounded for handles. Small stakes hold the wood from rolling off the ends and when loaded it may be conveniently handled by two persons.

COVERED SALT BOX.

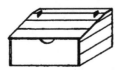

Animals will help themselves to salt if it is kept in a box like this. They soon find out how to lift the cover. Hinge the lid in such a way that it will drop of its own accord when the animal goes away. The opening in front should be about six inches wide and about four inches deep and the lid should project over the front edge of the box about an inch.

FEED MANGER FOR A GREEDY HORSE.

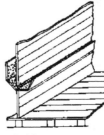

A box to induce a greedy horse to eat slowly is arranged through the partition with just a narrow opening at the bottom. You put the grain in the box on the outside of the partition and the horse gets it slowly. It saves grain and the horse takes more time to grind it.

POULTRY FEEDING BOX.

The box may be any length, according to the number of chickens to be fed and the length of the lumber available.

The box or feeder is twelve inches high in front and eighteen or twenty inches high at the back, with a width of six inches. The cover must be steep enough to prevent the chickens from roosting on it.

ONE-MAN SAW.

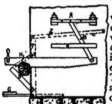

I have a device whereby one man can saw as much wood as two men could without it. It is rigged up at the end of the woodshed. The saw is outside, as shown in the drawing, and the spring with the projection that holds the log is inside. A is a cross-piece, supported by blocks, AA, which are nailed against the side of the building about eight feet up. There are three holes in this piece, so the hanger may be adjusted to the length of the saw. B is one inch thick, four inches wide and five feet long, with a hole at each end. This piece is split with a rip saw at the bottom end to receive the saw blade. C is a double slide to keep B from swinging sideways. D is a support to hold the log up to the proper height. E is a spring pole, made from a green sapling, about three inches through at the butt. F is a piece of two-by-four, with holes bored at intervals for the bolt H. H is an iron pin one inch in diameter and twelve inches long. G is a plank to stand on, one end of which rests on the ground and the other end on the lever which works the upright bar F.

LOG ROAD DRAG.

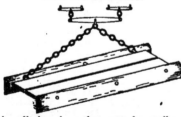

A split log drag that may be easily and quickly made is shown in the cut. The logs should be about twelve inches in diameter and six to eight feet long, split as near the middle as possible. If the wood is hard it will do good execution for some time without shoeing, but steel knife edges bolted to the edge of each log will do better work. The man who drives stands on the bottom boards, shifting his weight as required. The drag should be used often in spring time and early summer and after each rain storm.

CORN CHOPPER.

A trough about a foot wide and six or eight feet long, with a knife bolted as shown in the cut, makes a handy rig to chop ears of corn into short lengths for feeding. The knife may be made from a steel wagon tire.

NAIL BOX.

A nail box for holding two sizes of nails that is handy on every farm, is made by putting a center partition through the middle of the box. The partition should be about eight inches wide, which leaves room for a hand hole in the upper edge. Make the box big enough so it won't upset easily. About one foot wide and fourteen inches long with four inch sides is a good size.

ROOST AND NEST BOXES.

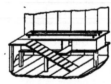

A good arrangement for heavy fowls is a set of nest boxes with roosts on top and an inclined board for the hens to walk up and down on. The nests are made large, about sixteen inches square and from sixteen to twenty inches high. The entrance to the nests is from the back and there is a runway at the back so the hens may enter any nest. There is also an entrance from the stairway in front as shown in the cut. The whole thing is made so it may be taken apart easily for cleaning.

FRUIT DRYER.

A splendid fruit dryer, and one that will not burn the fruit, is made of tin, with a space to hold water. The bottom and sides should be made of heavy tin, but a lighter grade will do for the top. It is filled about two-thirds full of water through a small opening in one corner. The evaporator is then placed on top of the kitchen range. It is better to spread butter over the top before putting fruit on. Drying apples are pared, cored and cut into rings with a paring machine. These rings wll dry in two or three hours and will be a very nice color. This evaporator is very nice for peaches or sweet corn. It takes corn five or six hours to dry, but it is very nice for winter use.

SMALL DIPPING TANK.

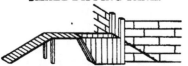

On a great many farms there are a few sheep, not enough to warrant the expense of a regular dipping tank, but too many to neglect. By placing a small tank just outside of a small yard as shown in the cut, two or three men can easily dip from twenty to fifty sheep. A dipping trough should lay on the platform draining back into the tank, and each sheep held in the trough for a few minutes to save the liquid.

FEED HOPPER.

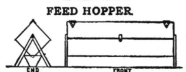

Procure a dry goods box one and one-half feet square and any length desired. Hang it lengthwise over a trough as shown in the cut. In the lower corner saw out an opening from a quarter to a half an inch wide, according to the kind of grain to be fed. It may be placed outdoors by extending the top boards roof fashion over the sides to prevent rain from running down and dripping into the trough.

RUN FOR SMALL CHICKENS.

Place two A tent coops opposite each other and connect them on the sides with fence panels of movable pickets. These picket fences are made by placing half lengths of lath one inch apart on 1x2 scantling twelve feet long. The fencing sections are placed so as to rest against the sides of the coops and kept together by laying

pieces across the top from one fence to another, with nails through the pieces to catch each fence. By using three coops, different sized yards and pens may be made.

COMBINED DOOR AND TABLE.

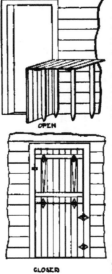

This door is not a door when it is made into a table. Two heavy strap hinges are needed on the bottom part for the door to swing on. The door is cut across at the height of an ordinary table and the two parts hinged together as shown. Legs are hinged to the upper cleat so they will swing out when the upper part of the door is let down. These leg hinges should play freely. Have a good wooden button to fasten the top of the door shut so it won't fall down when you are not looking.

BERRY CANE CUTTER.

A very handy cutter to trim berry bushes may be made out of an old shovel handle and the tip of a worn-out scythe. Cut the back of the scythe tip longer than the blade, so as to turn the point up. Saw a cut in the handle and insert the blade, and fasten with long rivets.

RACK FOR SEED CORN.

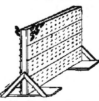

When it is desirable to test seed corn and to keep an accurate account of each ear there is no better plan than to stick the cobs on the points of wire nails that have been driven through a partition of inch boards. Each nail is numbered so that when the corn is tested a corresponding number in the testing box indicates the ear the grains were taken from. Ears of seed corn may be put on the rack in the fall and left without handling until time for testing and planting in the spring.

POULTRY DRINKING FOUNTAIN.

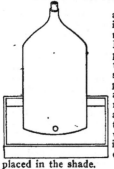

Take a gallon jug and drill a quarter-inch hole in one side near the bottom. Fill it with good pure water, cork tight and set in a shallow pan. The pan should be set on a block or box to raise it a few inches above the ground so that the chickens won't kick dirt into it. Use a box six or eight inches high, placed in the shade.

SAMPSON TO LIFT LOGS.

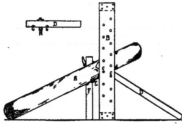

A sampson for raising trees or logs to be sawed or loaded is shown in the cut; (B) is a good solid hard wood plank 1½x8 inches by five feet long. There is another plank the same size, separated from (B) with cleats at top and bottom, leaving a two-inch space between for lever (D); (CC) are iron pins or bolts which fit easily in the holes bored through both planks three inches apart up and down and five inches apart sideways. A crotched limb on the opposite side of the log is marked (F); (E) is the end of a logging chain hooked into eye (H) on the lever. The chain is passed under the log and looped over the crotch of the stick; (GG) are notches in the lever (D) to hold the lever on the pins. To operate, place the plank upright edgeways to the log and leaning against it, put the crotched stick on the other side, adjust the chain and raise the log by working the

lever and moving the pins up one hole at a time. This device will raise a tree two feet through at the butt end, high enough to saw easily without a backache.

TO SHIP BEES ALIVE.

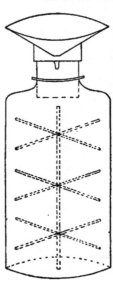

The post with cross arms in the bottle is to afford the bees a resting place to cluster, so the air may circulate around them. Otherwise they would lie solidly on the bottom and suffocate, as they cannot cling to glass. Each cross arm is fastened to the square post by one nail in the center. To insert in the bottle, the arms are turned parallel with the post and afterwards adjusted crosswise as shown in the cut. This kind of carrier is used principally for shipping bees for medical purposes. The poison from bee stingers has become an article of commerce and I have contrived this means of transporting the bees alive. The funnel is made of tin and is wide enough at the mouth to catch the bees shaken from a langstroth frame. It has a gate at the neck, so the bees are prevented from crawling out.

WINDOW VENTILATOR.

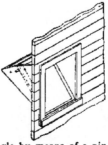

A splendid rig for ventilating a stable is made by building a three cornered box inside of the window opening. The sash is hinged at the bottom to swing in and is fastened at any angle by means of a pin through holes in the side of the box. V-shaped brackets at the side of the window will answer as well as the box but the box protects the glass when the window is open. This arrangement directs a current of air towards the ceiling where it may diffuse gradually without chilling the stable in any one spot. This is a good rig.

CARD BOARD CALIPERS.

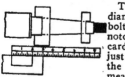

To measure the diameter of round bolts cut a square notch in a piece of card board until it just fits the round at the middle. Then measure the opening with a rule. This is a simple trick that may save a trip to the machine shop.

CORN CUTTING SLED.

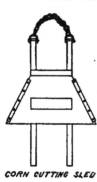

A sliding corn cutter, to be drawn by one horse, may be easily made by using two hardwood 4x4 pieces eight feet long, each rounded up in front for runners. A board platform is nailed very firmly on top of the runners, as shown in the cut. Old saw blades are bolted on the edges of the platform for knives. The saw blades should project at least two inches in order to cut through the larger stalks. A good, solid box is fastened to the floor for a seat. Two men ride upon the seat and gather the corn

CORN CUTTING SLED

as the knives cut it. When the men get as much corn as they can hold the horse stops and the corn is set up in shock. Be very careful, in using this implement, not to get cut with the knives. A good rule is never to step off in front or sideways.

COOP FOR LITTLE CHICKS.

This is a very light and cheap chicken coop that is easily made and is very convenient. Make two frames and hinge them together as shown and cover them with waterproof building paper. Two triangular frames are used for the front and back. The front frame is slatted across and the back frame is covered with paper. Both triangular frames are fastened to the main coop with staples and hooks. These coops may be folded together and packed away in little space.

TRAP NEST.

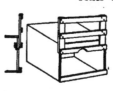

The nest box is twelve inches wide, twelve inches high, and fifteen inches long. The door is made of very light material and works easily in grooves. The door is held up by a hook so placed that when the door is lifted the hook drops away. This hook is placed so it will hold the door not quite high enough to let the hen pass through so that when she enters she lifts the door enough to release the hook. As she passes in the door drops and makes her a prisoner.

LAYING OUT THE GROUND FOR FOUNDATION WALLS—A203

YOU need eight good straight stakes and a long chalk line. Set the stakes as shown in the diagram and draw the chalk line taut. You can then dig right up to the corners without interfering with the stakes.

THE RULE OF SIX, EIGHT AND TEN.

In squaring the lines for the foundation of a building the following

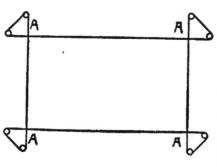

rule will be found very helpful. After the stakes are set and the chalk line drawn taut, take a ten-foot pole and measure off six feet from one corner on the line, stick a pin through the line to mark the place. Then on the other line measure eight feet from one corner and mark with a pin. If the distance is exactly ten feet between the two pins the corner is square.

ABOUT BARN ROOFS—A197.

CUT A 197 shows three ordinary roofs. The third pitch was the old style used almost universally a hundred years ago, shown at C. This gives mow room twelve feet deep at the peak above the plate line in a barn forty feet wide. The half pitch roof shown at D gives twenty feet mow room in the center above the plate, while the roof shown at E gives a height of twenty-four feet in the center and sixteen feet at FF. It will readily be seen that the value of such a roof is very much greater than either straight roof when it comes to storage capacity.

Besides the advantage of increased storage the larger roof is right when it comes to turning water. The upper part is not very steep. The upper roof is short and it is not necessary that it should be steep because there is very little accumulation of water. The lower portion of the roof drops away quickly. This is exactly the reverse of the old style lean-to where the addition sloped away and held a large amount of water to rot the shingles.

The advantage of a double roof pitch was never appreciated until horse forks came into general use to put hay and sheaves up into the loft in such quantities

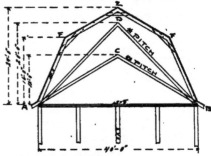

and so quickly that considerable storage room was found necessary in which to mow it away. Then again it requires from eight to ten feet headway to use a hay fork to advantage. In figuring the capacity of the different shaped roofs this fact should be taken into consideration.

It costs a little more to build a double roof, but the extra cost is not in proportion to the extra value. Then for a finish to a modern barn nothing will equal in appearance one of these double roofs when well built and rightly proportioned.

LINES FOR THREE HORSES.

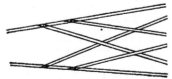

It is easy to make a set of lines and checks suitable for three horses simply by adding two long checks to the ordinary double lines as shown in the cut. Make the checks plenty long, because you need more room for three horses than you do for two. Often in hot weather, when working in the fields, you want to spread the horses as much as possible, and you must have long checks in order to do so.

THREE-HORSE EVENER.

To make a satisfactory three-horse evener to use on a pole make a solid iron brace out of a heavy wagon tire and bolt on top of the pole as shown in the cut. The distance of the draw bolt from the pole must be one-third of the length of the main draw bar, and this of

course must vary with the size of the horses and the length of whiffletrees. Usually the distance will be about twelve or fourteen inches. There should be a brace from the un-

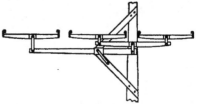

der side of the pole to the under side of the main brace and the draw bolt should go down through the strap and through the under brace. This arrangement is almost as handy to use as a common double tree and whiffletrees for two horses, because the brace supports the weight of the evener and it remains in place at all times. Some provision must be made for side draft, but that can usually be done according to the kind of machinery in use. Similar rigs are used on binders, but they apply equally as well to cutaway pulverizers, grain drills and many other farm implements.

Department of House Plans

OUR readers will understand that it would be useless for us to publish the following house designs unless we were also able to furnish the complete plans and specifications of the same so as to enable them to take advantage of the designs offered here to put them to practical use. For the accommodation of our readers, we have made special arrangements with the Radford Architectural Co., of Chicago, the largest architectural company in the world, to furnish us the complete plans and specifications of any one of these houses for the small price of $5.00. It is readily understood that this does not represent more than 10 per cent of the cost if it were designed and the plans made by a local architect. Their immense business enables them to furnish these plans at this small price.

Five-Room Cottage, No. A-2046.

A small but very neat little cottage house suitable for help on the farm may be built after this plan. It is a little affair, twenty-farms is because intelligent men are not willing to put up with the miserable accommodations that they find on most farms. They can

The complete plans and specifications of this house will be furnished for only five dollars.

two by thirty feet, and not very high up in the air, but it contains all the essentials of a good comfortable little home for a small family. It is exactly the sort of house to appeal to a young man recently married or about to be maried, just the kind of help that is most desirable and the most difficult to get and to keep.

The reason why good help is scarce on go to the nearby cities and rent little houses like this with conveniences where they can live in comfort and have a few luxuries. Now, the fact is, a house like this costs no more with proper management than the miserable make-shifts that you usually find for the use of tenants on farms all over the country. This cozy little combination of three rooms down stairs and two bed rooms and a bath room upstairs may be built for less than a thousand dollars; how much less depends upon local conditions and the

Here we have a front hall and a front stair that no young wife need be ashamed to show her best friends into, while upstairs we have

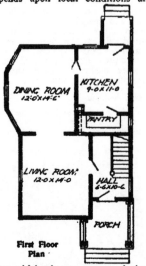

First Floor Plan

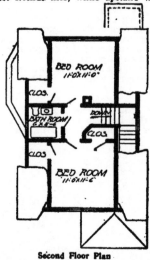

Second Floor Plan

extent to which the resources of the farm can help out. But the interest on a thousand dollars is only fifty or sixty dollars per year, and a good man is easily worth a bonus like that.

a good bath room and two good comfortable bed rooms that are light and airy and big enough to hold all the necessary furniture. Down stairs the house is a model of compactness and convenience for one so small.

Six-Room House, No. 2017.

For a larger house a very neat plan for six rooms and bath room is shown in this design.

It is almost perfect in regard to the arrangement of the rooms and the manner in which

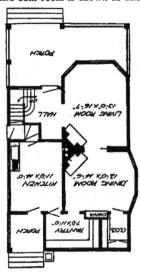

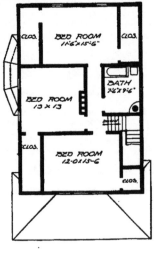

space is utilized to advantage. In fact, it would be difficult to put the same amount of building material together in any other form

from his own woodlot or stone piles, and to do his own teaming.

This style of house will never go out of

The complete plans and specifications of this house will be furnished for only five dollars.

to encompass so much comfort and convenience. It is especially well adapted to a farm where good help is kept. With such houses for men to live in there is no difficulty in keeping the kind of help needed.

It is difficult to estimate prices to apply to the different parts of the country, because the cost of materials and labor are very much greater in some sections than others, but probably from $1,400 to $1,700 may be given as a rough estimate. This, however, should be reduced considerably where a farmer is in position to supply a good deal of the material

style, because the front hall makes a pleasant entrance, the stairway looks well, there is a good-sized, convenient kitchen, a good pantry and a good dining room, all of which are necessary and permanently fashionable. And there are three comfortable bedrooms upstairs, besides a good bath room. If there is any good reason why a farmer should not take a bath it has never been publicly proclaimed. In addition the fine porch in front is attractive and pleasant in summer and the open fire places are comfortable, pleasant and healthful in cold weather.

Rough Cast House, No. 2035.

Another mode of building houses that is coming very much into fashion is the stucco material used for outside plastering. The idea is not new, in fact it dates back hundreds of years, but it has been recently revived because we have found out how to use cement to advantage in construction work of this kind. The modern outside cement plaster coat bears little or no relation to the old English rough cast work, which used to peel off in irregular patches and spoil the appearance of the building forever.

Another invention that has a great deal to do with the value of modern cement plaster work is the different kinds of expansion metal lath. Until cement mortar was troweled onto and into sheet metal lath it was impossible to provide against expansion and contraction. The best cement plaster on good metal lath will dry and hang free of cracks, but the same mixture spread on wooden lath will split and spider-leg in every direction.

It is easy when using material in a plastic condition to make good tight joints around window and door frames and to finish it with a neat workmanlike appearance. The final

no painting, which is another saving over a wooden house.

The complete plans and specifications of this house will be furnished for only five dollars.

dressing may be in any color and there are three general styles of finish—rough cast, pebbled and smooth. A house of this kind needs

This house has seven rooms besides the reception hall down stairs and a bath room upstairs. The smaller conveniences—such as pan-

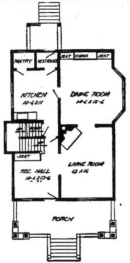

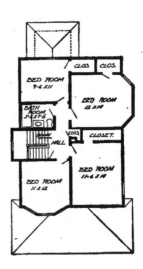

tries, china closet, back vestibule, with room for an ice box, and plenty of clothes closets—

have been worked out very carefully, as the plans show.

Cement Block House. No. 2034.

This house is thirty-one feet long by thirty-five feet wide, without measuring in the porches, and contains eight rooms, counting the reception hall as a room.

The first cement block houses were expensive and unsatisfactory because no one knew how to make the blocks or how to avoid the many little difficulties that always come along with new inventions. But mechanical ingenuity and the additional knowledge of mixing

tions where the block machine may be set down on the lot where the house is to be built and the gravel or sand for the blocks taken from the cellar excavation. In such cases the only teaming necessary is to haul the bags of cement, the mill work, joists and lumber necessary for the floors and the shingles and rafters for the roof.

The cellar wall may be made solid after the

The complete plans and specifications of this house will be furnished for only five dollars.

nuity and the additional knowledge of mixing cement, gravel, broken stone and cinders together to work right in the new improved block making machines, have simplified matters until it is now quite possible under favorable conditions to build a better house with cement blocks for less money than an ordinary wooden house of the same size and quality.

Of course, there are many side issues which affect this general statement. In some parts of the country the right kind of sand and stone is abundant. In other places it must be brought from a distance. In cement construction one of the greatest problems is the cost of teaming the heavy materials necessary to make the blocks, but there are other loca-

usual manner or it may be laid up with stone. In either case a course of cement mortar must be laid above grade line to prevent moisture from climbing up through the blocks in the upper wall.

One former difficulty which has now been overcome was the designing of cement blocks that fit around the windows and doors and that match right at the corners without making a whole lot of blocks of especial sizes. Before building a cement house it is better to read up on the subject and become thoroughly well posted.

A very strong point in favor of cement construction is the opportunity of making the cellar window sills of cement and to imbed the window frames thoroughly and carefully in the wall. A cellar under a farm house means a good deal to a farmer for the storage of fruits and vegetables, and the value of the

it is difficult to keep frost out unless windows may be shut tight and unless the frames fit close into the walls.

This is not a very large house, but it is a square built house which offers a good deal

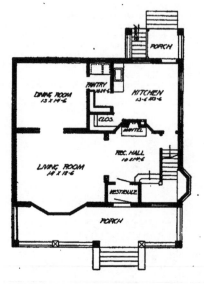

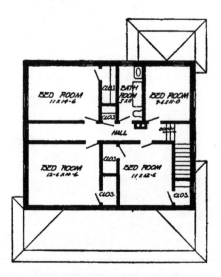

cellar is very much greater if the windows fit tight enough to control the temperature. It is easy to let in air by opening a window, but

of room, as will be seen by the floor plans the rooms are well laid out for elegance as well as comfort.

PRACTICAL HOUSE PLANS.

The following house designs are selected from among a great number with the idea of gathering the most practical and at the same time artistic houses that could be secured. They are all built on the sensible order, being as square as possible and doing away with the great amount of ginger bread work that has been quite prevalent in so many houses throughout the country. The tendency at the present time is to do away with the numerous ornaments and use instead dignified square corners. It gives a house a more substantial appearance and at the same time does not take away any of its attractiveness. Square houses are becoming more popular as there is less space wasted than in any other form of a house. It will also be noticed that the houses are equipped with good sized kitchens, for a

farm house without a kitchen would be as impractical as a stall without a feed box.

We have also endeavored to provide plans that contain suitable porch space, for every farm house should have some place where the occupants can enjoy in comfort their few spare hours. In pleasant weather, it is also a splendid place to entertain friends and often takes the place of a room, and in case of a large crowd they can overflow onto the lawn without any inconvenience to anyone.

All these things should be taken into consideration before a house is built, as with most people it is the event of a life-time and should therefore be given serious consideration. It is just as easy to have things so arranged that some comfort can be secured without adding very considerably to the cost, if only a little judgment and forethought is used in selecting the plan.

Design No. A-1163

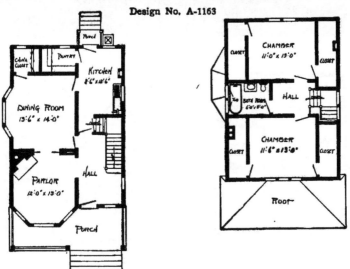

The complete plans and specifications of this house will be furnished for only five dollars.

Design No. A-1520

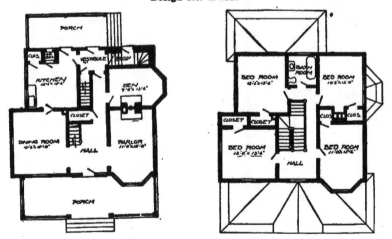

The complete plans and specifications of this house will be furnished for only five dollars.

Design No. A-1019

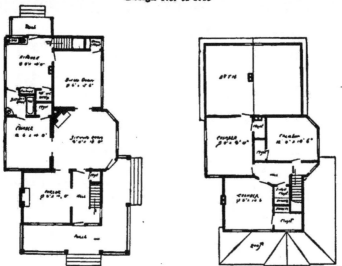

The complete plans and specifications of this house will be furnished for only five dollars.

Design No. A-1083

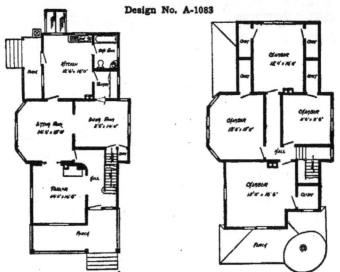

The complete plans and specifications of this house will be furnished for only five dollars.

Lightning Source UK Ltd.
Milton Keynes UK
UKHW021857280620
365591UK00013BA/489